DR MOFO[...]

FLOURISHING FORTIES

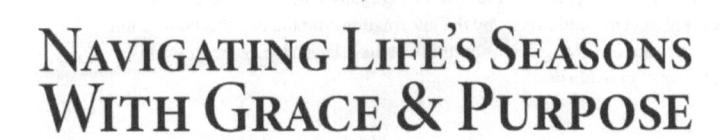

Navigating Life's Seasons With Grace & Purpose

First Published 2024 by Dr Mofoluwaso Ilevbare

Published by Dr Mofoluwaso Ilevbare

Produced by Indie Experts
indieexpertspublishing.co.nz

Copyright © Dr Mofoluwaso Ilevbare 2024

The moral right of the author to be identified as the author
of this work has been asserted.

All rights reserved. Except for the purposes of reviewing, no part of this publication may be reproduced or transmitted in any form or by any means, electronic or mechanical, including photocopying, recording or any information storage or retrieval system, without the written permission of the author. Infringers of copyright render themselves liable for prosecution.

Cover design and typesetting by
Ammie Christiansen, Fast Forward Design
fastforwarddesign.co.nz
Typeset in 11pt Minion Pro

ISBN:
978-1-7637039-0-2 (Printed)
978-1-7637039-1-9 (eBook)

Disclaimer:
Every effort has been made to ensure this book is as accurate and complete as possible, however they may be errors both typographical and in content. The author and the publisher shall not be held liable or responsible to any person or entity with respect to any loss or damage caused or alleged to have been caused directly or indirectly by the information contained in this book. Some names and identifying details in this book have been changed to protect the privacy of individuals.

"To women over 40 everywhere – Be Unstoppable!"

Contents

Introduction 1
Definitions 8
PART ONE Spring: Change is Inevitable 9
Chapter 1: The End or the Beginning 11
Chapter 2: Accepting Change 19
#1: Application Exercise: The Recall 30
Chapter 3: Removing the Mask We Wear 33
#2: Application Exercise: The Unveiling 40
#3: Application Exercise: It's over to you now: 43
#4: Application Exercise: Who's Shaped Your Life: 46
PART TWO Summer: New Beginnings 49
Chapter 4: Now you're Adulting 51
#5 Application Exercise: F.R.E.S.H. Start 59
Chapter 5: Purpose and Vision 63
#6 Application Exercise: Check-In 71
Chapter 6: Charting Your Path 73
#7 Application: Vision Unleashed 80
Chapter 7: The Big Aunties –Now I'm One of Them 83
#8 Application Exercise: Ageism 89

Chapter 8: Change is Here 91

#9 Application Exercise: Coping with Change.................................94

Chapter 9: Embracing Change 97

#10 Application Exercise: Pushing Season 101

Chapter 10: Failing Forward... 103

#11 Application Exercise: The Wake-Up Call................................. 110

Chapter 11: Managing the Blues 111

#12: Application Exercise: Check-In 119

PART THREE Autumn: Thriving Still.. 121

Chapter 12: Equipped for Every Season.. 125

Chapter 13: Transform Your Habits, Transform Your Life......... 131

#13 Application Exercise: Reframing Perceived Weaknesses 141

Chapter 14: Investing in Your Energy... 143

Chapter 15: You're in the Driver's Seat Now 155

PART FOUR Winter: Build for NEXT.. 165

Chapter 16: Laws of Nature 167

Note from the Author.. 177

ONE LAST THING… 180

Introduction

"You are not behind! Start showing up for the life you deserve" – Mofoluwaso Ilevbare

Hey Beautiful,

I am glad you picked up this book. Something about it caught your attention, and I am keen to hear your story. So, grab a cup of tea or a smoothie, find a quiet and cozy spot, and let us have a heart-to-heart conversation here and now.

If you are over 35, research suggests that 95% of who you are today is an accumulation of thought patterns, learned behaviour, and unconscious habits already wired in your brain over time. This means that the way you speak, behave and think, and the things you do are mostly predictable, but thanks to the neuroplastic nature of the brain, you can choose to unlearn, relearn, and reprogram your brain with new habits and thought patterns that can serve who you truly are and who you are going to become.

I loved my 20s and rocked my 30s. People who grew up with me would describe me as energetic, organized, and ambitious. As I became a woman in her 40s, I started to notice a shift. My body was changing. My perspectives, too. My social circles evolved, and so did my priorities. I began to attach a new level of importance to every day when I opened my eyes and got out of bed. It was as if my mind knew it was time to stop wasting precious time watching others live their lives. If you feel the same way, this is the book for you.

In quiet moments, whenever I reflected on life after 40, my mind would paint a picture of deciduous trees – those trees that shed their leaves annually in response to environmental changes. For the tree to thrive in each season, it requires different positioning, preparation, and presentation. Just as a deciduous tree responds to the seasons – spring, summer, autumn, and winter – figuratively, we all experience life in these seasons, too.

- **Spring** connotes newness, a fresh start, rejuvenation, and a burst of energy. Spring can also be interpreted as a period of anxiety when you are birthing something new and hope it will grow.

- **Summer** connotes blooming, a season of fruitfulness, vibrancy, and luxury. Summer can also mean hot temperatures and unbearable stickiness in life.

- **Autumn:** In some parts of the world, autumn is also commonly referred to as fall. This season can sometimes feel like a time of drift, dryness and disruption.

- **Winter:** connotes a time of hardship, nakedness, living life on bare bones, a time of vulnerability and exposure which may lead to death if specific mitigation actions are not taken. As winter blows harder, deciduous trees are forced to retreat into dormancy.

As you transition into your 40s, 50s, and beyond, one decade fades and another begins. Only this time, you must be truly present and in charge. You cannot blame anyone else for the actions you will take or are taking now. Why? Because once you are 40+, you are expected to be a grown woman. Life assumes you have learned some good or some hard-knock lessons and have found what truly brings you joy...but have you, really?

In the harsh seasons, a deciduous tree looks deserted and exposed, as if it has lost its purpose, but after a little while, new leaves sprout, and it blooms again. **In case you are feeling like that tree in its desolate moments, I wrote this book so you can navigate your seasons with grace and purpose.**

Enjoying the fullness of each season

To fully enjoy the seasons of life in your 40s, I'd like you to pay attention to these five critical stages on your journey to flourishing.

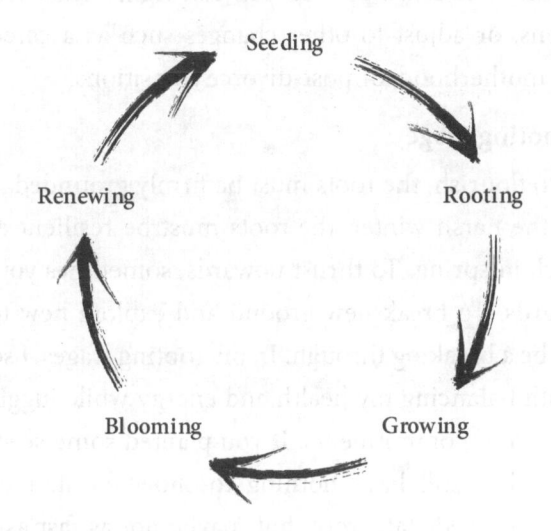

```
        Seeding
    ↗           ↘
Renewing        Rooting
    ↑             ↓
Blooming  ←    Growing
```

Stage 1: Seeding Stage

I currently work in the flour milling and baking sector. Once, I visited a wheat farmer to understand how wheat is planted and harvested before it is converted to flour. As we walked through acres of wheat, we discussed two critical components in a seed: the protoplasm (the living cell inside the seed) and the cytoplasm (responsible for the living part of the cell). When a seed is planted in good soil and watered, the protoplasm and cytoplasm are activated, and the germination process kicks in. Without a good seed, the right amount of moisture and good soil, there can be no promise or hope for a flourishing tree. Your thoughts are seeds. Your goals are seeds. Your dreams and visions are seeds. To flourish maximally over 40, get your seed right. Get your core right. Whether you are a busy mother on the go or embracing a new sense of independence, this may be another chance to separate good seeds from the bad seeds of the past – past hurts, past pain, past disappointments, bad decisions, and unhealthy relationships – so you can right some wrongs, find new passions, or adjust to other changes such as a career switch, relocation, motherhood, or post-divorce transitions.

Stage 2: Rooting Stage

For a tree to flourish, the roots must be firmly grounded. For a tree to survive the harsh winter, the roots must be resilient enough to bounce back in spring. To thrust upwards, sometimes you've got to go downwards. To break new ground and explore new territories, there must be a breaking through. In my rooting stages, I sometimes struggle with balancing my health and energy while juggling work, family, and other commitments. If you planted some seeds in your 20s and 30s but still have nothing to show for it, I can relate. Sometimes, the seeds take root, but maybe not as fast as you want them to. I have learned that in the many waiting periods of my life, which felt like the rooting stage, some of the seeds I had sown were silently growing, new prongs were searching for water, feeding on nutrients, penetrating the ground, strengthening the foundation on which I would eventually grow stronger. Sometimes, I have had to close a chapter and accept some non-returns. Focus on nourishing your roots so they can last and serve you well. As you put in the work needed for your transformation, remember to be patient through this process.

Stage 3: Growing Stage

A visible sign of a flourishing life is growth! If a seed is planted in hard soil, that seed may not grow, or when it does, the growth is stunted because the roots find it hard to penetrate. If the soil is moist and rich with fertilisers, the roots penetrate quicker and gain ground, leading to good growth. The quality of what is hidden under the soil determines the health and wellness of what eventually appears on the surface. Equally, external positive reinforcements keep the plant growing. As I experienced personal and professional growth, I struggled to keep up with some relationships. Soon, I caught myself pretending to laugh in forums that no longer served the woman I was becoming and feeling miserable for saying yes in situations when I should have said no, all because I didn't want to ruffle feathers. I found it hard to express to people that a transformation was taking place inside me. I stayed in the same circles, trying to *show face*, pretending I was still the old me they could depend on.

At some point, I embraced the new me and courageously shared who I was becoming. I embraced the liberation of saying no. I streamlined my circle, was mindful of where I spent my energy, and accepted what was out of my control (people's opinions and expectations). Over time, I have developed systems and habits that serve my next level. As your "hard shell" breaks through, there can be sprouting of new thoughts, new ideas, new openings, and new visions in your 40s.

Instead of dreading what you may be losing, embrace the newness and go from shyness to showing up.

Stage 4: Blooming Stage

Where there is good growth, trees bloom well. If your internal and external environments are toxic, nothing good can bloom. What a joy when flowers bloom, and everything in your life feels beautiful and just about right. I've been there too. My finances are amazing. My husband is as loving as ever. My kids make me proud. Work is going well, and I am recognized on global platforms for my impact. In the blooming stage, everything seems to be going well. What a beautiful time that is. You wish it could remain that way for a hundred more years.

Are you in that season of life? If yes, are you truly enjoying each moment and soaking it all in? I hope you are. When a tree blooms and fruit appears, it is attractive to others. Kids want to throw sticks to pluck the fruits. Farmers spend time harvesting the fruits to sell and make money. Customers line up in shops to buy good fruit. However, when you're fruiting, the branches are heavier, and the tree needs more core strength to sustain it. If the roots are not strong on the day of adversity, the tree loses its stamina and dies easily.

Stage 5: Renewal Stage

No matter how beautiful your lawn is, at some point, you have to tidy it up. I find the renewal stage as a time to shed dead leaves – bad habits and stale thinking that no longer serves the new you. The renewal stage is a time to live with courage and prune your branches – renew your network, realign your priorities, restock and rediscover yourself. I wrote this book to inspire women like me who are juggling so many things in life while also going through these different stages.

It is the paradox of life – a season will end and give way to another. In my 40s, I have chosen to embrace the woman I am and hope to become more of who I was created and called to be. If this resonates with you, I invite you to take a journey with me through the pages of this book.

You will find stories you can relate to, practical advice that saves you time and offers tangible results, and an uplifting zing that makes you thrive through your 40s, 50s, 60s, and beyond.

I hope, like me, you find the courage and strength to reassess your 40s and choose to be a flourishing woman with better health, stronger relationships, and a sharper purpose in life.

Welcome to your next level. Forty isn't old—it's your journey to being bold!

It's time to *flourish*.

Dr Mofoluwaso Ilevbare

Definitions

Flourish

/ˈflʌrɪʃ/

to be in one's prime; be at the height of fame, excellence, influence, etc. (Dictionary.com)

verb: *flourish*; **present participle:** *flourishing*
- to grow luxuriantly, or thrive in growth, as a plant (www.merriam-webster.com)
- to reach a height of development or influence

noun: *flourish*; **plural noun:** *flourishes*
- a bold or extravagant gesture or action made especially to attract attention
- an impressive and successful act or period

PART ONE
Spring: Change is Inevitable

The Courage to Fly

Everything with a beginning has an end
and the end of one is the beginning of another.
Inside everything that exists today is something incomplete.
Inside every seed are thousands of potential trees.

The ability to evolve lies in every caterpillar.
But until the desire to fly outweighs the security of the cocoon,
The threads stay intact, never to break.

Imagine a butterfly flapping away, so merry
Big and bold blue, red or yellow spotted wings
The world may never know the strength you carry
Till you spread your wings, and let courage fly.

© *Mofoluwaso Ilevbare*

CHAPTER 1:
The End or the Beginning

"In the cycle of life, an ending carries within it the potential of new horizons and fresh beginnings" – Mofoluwaso Ilevbare

I had felt something like a little pimple on my bum but thought it was nothing. From Monday to Thursday, I went to work ignoring the pain and slight swelling. By Friday morning, the pain was so excruciating I could hardly sit comfortably in meetings. I finished work early that day and headed for the hospital. On arrival, I explained my issue to the nurse and waited to see a doctor. After a physical examination, the doctor slashed the pimple open, drained the infection, bandaged my bum, and advised me to take a painkiller if the need arose. Then she handed me some ointment and confirmed an appointment for the following week.

I thanked the doctor and left, sceptical about not being given any antibiotics. The pain worsened over the weekend, so on Monday morning, I returned to the hospital. After an examination, the doctor suggested various tests and I obliged. At that moment, I was at their mercy.

I couldn't tell which pain was heavier: the pain in my buttocks or the one I felt swelling in my chest. I was angry that I hadn't been given antibiotics which would have helped avoid this escalation. After another three doctors examined me, and I underwent blood checks, a scan and an MRI, I waited anxiously for some news.

By around 8 p.m., I was hungry, wondering when I could go home and be with my family. Finally, a whole team of doctors came into the waiting room looking serious. One asked me in French if I had any family in Geneva… Their questions put me on high alert and tension rose up through my spine. My mind started racing, and fear gripped me.

"We have to take you into the theatre for an emergency procedure. We would like to perform the surgery tonight." This all seemed to come out in a rush from the French specialist.

The doctor who had treated me three days earlier might have been thankful not to be near me at that moment as I wanted her to feel the full weight of my anger. I was angry because I thought the situation had become complicated because she had made an avoidable mistake. Now I was being scheduled for an emergency procedure. But I was also scared as I looked around at the empty room. I thought of my husband, my 11-month-old baby and his brother. What was I going to do?

I called my husband, who immediately rushed down to the hospital with our children, and with his consent, I was prepped for surgery and taken into the theatre. The doctors had confirmed that the infection had a very high toxicity level, and something had to be done fast to contain it. Moments before being wheeled into the theatre, the doctor who attended to me the week before appeared, sounding shocked and apologetic at the same time. All I felt was anger towards her. I blamed her for not giving me antibiotics. I blamed her for her negligence. In fact, I blamed her for everything.

As I was being wheeled into the theatre, scenes of my life replayed in my head like a fast swipe through an archive of memories. I cried as I hugged my husband and tried to be brave for my boys.

As I gained full consciousness a few hours later, I first noticed I could barely move due to the excruciating pain. I was in isolation, my quarantine apparent from the yellow skeleton-head hazard stickers splashed on the walls and door. The nurse and doctor were covered from head to toe in protective clothing. It was not long before I found out I was suspected of having Ebola virus or something else they couldn't yet figure out – but it was definitely very serious.

In the coming days I had visits from specialists in microbiology, virology, and disease control. They came in, discussed my case, tried to resolve the antibiotics that were not working and work out the next line of action. My symptoms were inconsistent with Ebola, which only confused them more. Nobody was allowed to visit. I was glad I could at least hear my babies' voices and their dad over the phone from time to time. I was meant to be relieved that I was in safe hands, but it didn't feel that way. It felt strange and cold being alone. Here I was again walking through the valley of the shadow of death for the third time in six years.

Somewhere after 15 days post-surgery, it seemed nothing was happening. So much talking was going on about me and around me, but none of it made sense. All I knew was that I wasn't well yet and might never be again. The toxins in my bloodstream were highly concentrated, and the medical team needed to manage it carefully.

The doctors asked me if I had visited Africa or the United States in the previous six months. My answer was yes, as I had been to West Africa for a family vacation and had honoured a few speaking engagements in the United States during that time. As the hours rolled into days and the days piled up, I could feel my strength draining away. I felt too weak to move or even fight back. My spirit was angry within me, struggling so hard to stay alive, and I could feel it to my core. I had restless sleep and heart palpitations.

I asked my husband to send my laptop over to the hospital. When I received it, I put together a YouTube playlist of every sermon or encouraging song I could find around healing, faith, and hope from preachers like Kenneth Hagin, Kathryn Kuhlman, T. D. Jakes, and Joyce Meyer. The warrior woman inside of me wanted to fight back. It was time to be unstoppable. I composed positive affirmations and health declarations, which I repeated to myself morning, night, and noon, mustering the words with all the strength I had left. I had decided to do everything I possibly could to live again. My laptop screensaver was the last picture I took with my family. I had to get back to them.

I asked one of the nurses to move my hospital bed closer to the window. At first, she struggled with the idea, but I convinced her. I couldn't sit up by myself, but by using the hospital bed lever, I could catch a glimpse of the sunrise. I wanted this badly because deep down, I believed that as long as I could watch the sun rise and set, it would remind me of God holding the universe together, giving me hope that I would get out of the hospital alive. Every night I looked outside to catch a glimpse of the moon or the starry sky. As I did, I remembered the quote, "The darkest nights hold the brightest stars." Every morning at dawn, I would utter these words under my breath: "As *the sun rises every morning, my body regains daily strength. I rise like the sun, stronger and unstoppable, every day.*"

Your thoughts can control your life. Change your thinking if you want to change your life. Be conscious of what you allow into your heart/mind. Guard your heart. Really guard it. The real *you* resides there. Courage resides there. Peace resides there.

Gradually, I felt more faith rise in my spirit, and my inner resolve strengthened. After a few days, the doctors told me that my health was slowly improving. The antibiotics were working, and my bloodwork had returned to normal. Every day was another victory step in the battle for my strength and recovery. Every evening, my husband would call to pray for me and encourage me. I missed him so much, and my boys missed me too, but they had to stay away until I was in the clear. I also figured out that by the time I got back home, my 11-month-old baby would probably be fully weaned from my breastfeeding. The days were long, and the nights felt longer, but approximately 31 days after I set foot in that hospital, I was given a clean bill of health and declared free to go home.

Could it be true? Was I finally healed and free?

I sat on the bed for a while, looking around the room as the nurse came around to bid me goodbye. My heart was bursting with gratitude too deep to express in words. With tears streaming down my face, I stood up from the bed, had my final bed bath, and packed my bag. At that moment, I chose not to call my husband to pick me up. He knew I was likely to be discharged that day but didn't know exactly when. Apparently, he had dressed up the boys, waiting for the doctor's call so they could pick me up and welcome me home.

Over 30 days, mostly in isolation, but alive again. I wanted to soak it all in. I walked out of the main hospital area, greeted by the beautiful rays of the sun. I took a deep breath, looked at the sky, and spread my hands wide. I removed my shoes and walked around the hospital garden, feeling the earth underneath my feet and grateful to be standing upright instead of lying in a morgue. Passers-by stared from a distance, but it didn't bother me. *You never truly value what you have until you lose it.* After a few minutes, which may have been roughly half an hour, I picked up my bag and flagged down a cab. It was time to go home.

As I approached my 40s, I remembered each of the three occasions on which my life was most at risk. I have had three major crises, which I call near-death experiences, though they weren't what is commonly understood by that term. The thoughts made me more grateful to be alive, and they awakened in me a deeper desire to make a difference with the gift of life I had been given again, and to help others value it more.

I've spoken to many others who have experienced a similar situation that catalysed change in their lives. Many things can happen at any time, be it an illness, the loss of a friend when young and unexpected, or a family emergency. But you don't have to wait for a catastrophic experience before you review your life and assess what truly matters. Think about the life you have lived so far and take a moment to reflect on one or more of these questions:

Looking back over my life, what significant highs and lows did I encounter?

What situations made me feel truly content?

What habits and way of thinking have I graduated from?

Am I taking life for granted or living it to the fullest?

If given the chance to go back in time, would I change my current track or keep going?

You may also choose to do a life mapping exercise – the template is available in the Flourishing Forties Collective vault on our website, flourishingforties.com.

Let's go deeper.

Chapter 2:
Accepting Change

"To everything there is a season, a time for every purpose under heaven" – Ecclesiastes 3:1

Growing up, I loved birthdays but I remember waking up one day and the first thought that came to mind was *"Who moved my age?"* It was another birthday, and the calendar does not lie. I felt like Hem and Haw, characters in Spencer Johnson's book, *Who Moved My Cheese?*[1], who struggle to navigate change and locate their cheese.

In the Bridges Transition Model[2], a well-known change management tool used in human resources, American organizational consultant William Bridges explains that personal and psychological response to change occurs in three phases:

1. Endings
2. Neutral zone
3. New beginnings

---

1 *Who Moved My Cheese?* by Spencer Johnson
2 https://wmbridges.com/about/what-is-transition/

In the ending zone, you go through a rollercoaster of emotions related to letting go, which can present as resistance, fear, anxiety, loss, rejection, or even depression. Letting go of comfortable situations, titles that have given you security, items you value dearly, or people in your circle, can be challenging.

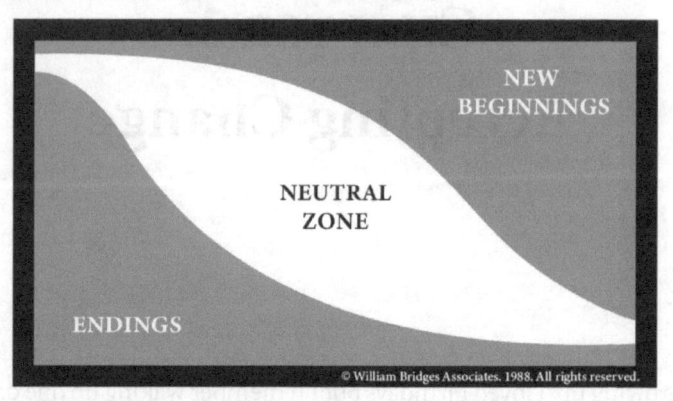

[Diagram: A curve showing transition from ENDINGS through NEUTRAL ZONE to NEW BEGINNINGS. © William Bridges Associates. 1988. All rights reserved.]

The neutral zone is a bridge between what used to be and what could possibly be. This can be a season of scepticism, confusion, uncertainty and instability. In contrast, it could also be a season of positive anticipation, renewed energy, and vitality.

"What is happening to me?"

"What will the next phase of my life look like?"

"What opportunities are likely to come my way?"

When I was eight years old, one of the ways my primary school teacher taught us about metamorphosis was through a class experiment where every one of us planted beans or maize seeds in a small tin. We were instructed to water the soil and document our daily observations. I remember feeling frustrated after Day 3. With swollen cheeks and sunken shoulders, I cried to my mother, saying, "Nothing is growing. My seed is dead." She calmed me down and told me to be patient and learn to wait. For an eight-year-old child, the word "wait" does not exist. *Waiting for 60 seconds could seem like forever.*

After a few more days, I screamed in excitement when I saw a breaking in the soil and something green shooting out. Very rapidly, that little seed blossomed into a plant with lush, green leaves and fresh branches for a while. My joy could not be contained. When you plant a seed in the ground and water it every day, it looks for a while like nothing is happening. Change is what you see on the outside. Transition is what goes on *inside*. The quality of change is massively influenced and shaped by what goes on inside anything.

What do you do when you are in-between?

Don't despise your season of being *in-between*. I liken it to the period of silent growth as the roots of the bean seed search and penetrate the soil that surrounds it, in the hope that it will be good ground for transformation and stability for the potential bean tree. The *process* of growth is necessary. If you stick with the process, your budding will appear.

The **new beginnings zone** is the third phase in the Bridges model.

New beginnings do not always mean things will look beautiful, attractive and fresh on the outside. A new beginning could be like a fresh *wound* because you just narrowly escaped death, or like a tree whose branches have just been pruned, so that it can grow properly. Embracing new beginnings takes courage; for you, it could be a step into the unfamiliar.

Accepting Change and Ageing

It is difficult to define exactly what successful ageing means, but we know it goes beyond just physical and mental health. Research undertaken by Brunton and Scot[3] (2015) documented that many people experience what is called ageing anxiety, which could be triggered by the fear of old people, fear of losing something or someone, and a myriad of psychological concerns. Coping with the psychological and physical changes that come with ageing is like accepting change. Your self-esteem, personal growth, attitude towards life, fears, hopes, and dreams, and purposefulness, all contribute to successful ageing. Many women told me that by the time you hit 40, you stop giving a hoot about all the little dramas of life. About time, isn't it?

Expectations and Hope for the 40s

As a teenager, I looked forward to growing older. We were always surrounded by family members, some of whom lived with us for a while. Watching my big aunties and uncles finishing school, looking good in work suits, buying beautiful cars and living in lovely houses was inspiring. I would daydream of being able to do my own thing, have my own money, and spending it on whatever luxury I wanted. I wanted a lot – like driving the latest posh car, living in a big house I owned, and having the kind of tight-knit, fun-loving family I saw on family TV classics. As I grew into an adult, I started to live my dreams but also realized that not all that glitters is gold.

---

3 Brunton, R. J., & Scott, G. (2015). Do We Fear Ageing? A Multidimensional Approach to Ageing Anxiety. Educational Gerontology, 41(11), 786–799. https://doi.org/10.1080/03601277.2015.1050870

Among the Baby Boomer and Gen X generations, reaching the age of 40 was rated as significant. It still is in many quarters. Plenty of women approach it with a feeling of anxiety or excitement. I was one of the very excited ones. I had a massive fortieth birthday celebration with family, friends, and some celebrities. The event made the news as I also announced the intent to start flourishing forties. Then, a little while after turning 40, one of the first things I noticed was an unexplainable weight gain. In two years, I gained so much weight without significantly changing my health habits. I could not understand why no matter what I tried, how hard I exercised, how long I fasted, what diet challenge I picked up, I seemed to add a 0.5kg every fortnight or so.

At first, I avoided the situation. Then I moved to judging myself. I started comparing myself to the beautiful slim figures of colleagues and influencers over 40 that flooded my social media feed, and gradually my thoughts went downhill into finally having to accept it was my fate and genes. It was a while before I snapped out of that state and booked an appointment with my GP to figure out what was going on! I found out the weight gain was caused by hormonal imbalance, which could be managed. Only then did my flourishing season begin – embracing my body, loving the woman I am becoming, taking ownership of actions to bounce back to health, and starting to operate on a whole new level.

When I interviewed several women in their 40s, some of the phrases I heard them blurt out sounded like:

- I am grateful I have achieved [this or that]…
- I am excited and super pumped!
- I haven't been able to do [this or that]…
- This is not who I thought I would become…

- When did I get so old?
- There's no big deal about turning 40...
- It's time to start planning for my next 40 years.
- What's a crazy thing I could do, now that I'm 40?

In writing this book, I have been thinking about the unique awesomeness of each generation. When older generations speak about millennials and Gen Zs,[4] they usually speak about them like a special breed that dropped from the sky (or maybe even a different planet). Their thinking, mannerisms, language, and attitude to life and work feel different from those of earlier generations. The major differentiators are the phenomena that characterise the season in which they were born. Every generational season is characterised by different circumstances which alter our outlook.

Generations	Born	Current Age
Gen Z	1997-2012	11-26
Millennials	1981-1996	27-42
Gen X	1965-1980	43-58
Boomers II (aka Generation Jones)*	1955-1964	59-68
Boomers I *	1946-1954	69-77
Post War	1928-1945	78-95
WWII	1922-1927	96-101

https://www.beresfordresearch.com/age-range-by-generation/

People in their 40s have unique circumstances that can influence their season. People in their 60s or 70s I spoke to while writing this

---

4 https://www.beresfordresearch.com/age-range-by-generation/

book sometimes expressed that they find people in their 40s weird too. This is because of the significant paradigm shift in our mindset and vision. Remember when we thought turning 40 was the end of youthfulness? Decades ago, anyone in their 40s was considered "mid-life"; most would already be thinking about retirement, pension and legacy. In some cultures, women would be expected to have settled into marriage or motherhood, dressing differently, and gradually winding down in their ambitions.

Now here we are, and it does not feel that old after all. Today, women in their 40s are defying odds, kickstarting dreams, becoming self-made billionaires, rewriting new scripts, going forward (not back) to school, evolving in new ways. and living healthier. The kinds of decisions "forticians" (people in their 40s), as I like to call them, make are indicative of the millennial outlook. After all, the oldest millennial is in their early 40s already in 2023.

The oldest millennials are in their early forties already in 2023.

Influenced by globalisation and, increasingly, the rise of artificial intelligence and economic disruption, forticians are making smarter and better choices to look after their health, wealth, and relationships; becoming tech savvy; and being role models for Gen Zs. Staying loyal to one company till retirement is rapidly becoming an obsolete concept. Waiting to retire before enjoying life now feels foreign. The new generation of forticians are measuring life not solely on age but on capacity, impact, growth, and contribution to something bigger than themselves. The old retirement and pension goals have been replaced with phrases like "dying empty", "leaving a legacy", "lasting for my family and purpose", "living limitless", and more.

Yet, turning 40 still weighs heavily on many minds. For some of us, our 40s come with unexpected shifts that can feel slightly overwhelming – from wondering whether you are experiencing perimenopause or just feeling deflated, to racing against time like there's not enough of you to go round everyone else. It is easier to feel isolated.

Six Categories of Forticians

1. Bring it on! You are excited for the big 4-0. You feel mentally ready to take on the new season. Like a tree welcoming new shoots in spring, your branches are almost screaming "Welcome, I'm glad to carry you."

2. It's over! You are not enthusiastic about turning 40. The weight of losing out on certain freedoms and flexibility makes you feel that part of your life is over for good.

3. It's got to be perfect! You're excited to celebrate the big 4-0 and based on stories you've heard or experiences you've had, you are determined to make this season of your life perfect at all costs.

4. I'm old! You are overwhelmed with anxiety and disappointment that you will not have certain opportunities anymore because of your age. Maybe you have some regrets about past actions that have led you to where you are right now.

5. So what? You wonder why there is so much fuss about being 40. For you, it's not that deep – only an age in the calendar.

You don't intend to make any drastic changes to your life, nor make any fuss about this season.

6. What's my purpose? Like scales falling off your eyes, you feel behind and realise you've got to make your life mean something, but you lack clarity on exactly what that is and where to begin.

Handling Regrets

In a TED Talk, American journalist Kathryn Schultz[5] shared her regret about getting a tattoo and managing the emotions that came afterwards. She emphasised that instead of beating yourself up over a regret, acknowledge your imperfections and extend forgiveness to yourself for past mistakes. People who say they have no regrets... is that really what they are saying, or do they mean that, with hindsight, they couldn't have done it differently?

Let's keep it real! Life is full of choices. Some choices lead to expected destinations while some bring a tale of woe. Instead of living in a world of should have, could have, would have or have nots, choose to accept the experience that failure or disappointment or regret taught you as a nudge for better decisions. If you learned nothing in the process, you wasted an experience. Like Schultz expressed so beautifully, *"The goal is not to live a life of no regrets, but to accept that we all have flaws and can improve."* One of the signs that we acted out of season is the regret of missed opportunities and the damage we suffer for being distracted or blind to the things that

---

5 https://www.ted.com/talks/kathryn_schulz_on_being_wrong?

mattered the most at that time. This understanding should guide how you think about your age and the seasons of your life.

Are Your Regrets Holding You Back?

Everyone has something they regret. Whenever I find myself thinking "If only", I know I have two choices. I can choose to replay the scenario over and over in my mind, feeling sorry or angry, or I can let it go so it does not keep pulling me back. Is there a situation you look back on now and wish things had gone differently? Does the memory still give you jitters? Have you forgiven yourself or the other person in that situation yet? Regrets are usually linked to decision-making, and making decisions is a big part of life, or else we end up "coasting" through life without ambition, which is a choice and decision in itself. In a 2011 study[6] that surveyed a group of Americans, people felt more regretful about actions they did not take than those they took. In the same study, women had common regrets about relationships and love, while men had more regrets about work or career. Interesting outcome, isn't it? If you find yourself constantly drained by regrettable moments in your present life, ask yourself if it will really matter five years from now.

Instead of living in a world of should have, could have, would haves or have nots, choose to accept the experience that failure or disappointment or regret taught you as a nudge for better decisions.

---

6 Regrets of the Typical American: Findings From a Nationally Representative Sample - Mike Morrison, Neal J. Roese, 2011 (sagepub.com)

The 40s are a unique period in life for a reset, renewed clarity, and intentional planning. A time to forgive. A time to heal. A time to grow. A time to pursue. Get out of your own head and out of your own way. Take your place and get back on track. It's time to make this your best decade so far!

#1: Application Exercise: The Recall

Find a quiet moment, grab your journal and pen, and spend the next 5 minutes with me:

1. A painful experience that has made me stronger is …

_____

_____

_____

2. One lesson I've learnt through success is …

_____

_____

_____

3. One lesson I've learnt through failure is …

_____

_____

_____

4. Starting tomorrow, what is one thing you can do to make the version of yourself in 10 years super proud of you. Start with "I would..."

_____

_____

_____

5. As you transition into your 40s, a guiding *word* for this decade would be

_____

_____

_____

Chapter 3:
Removing the Mask We Wear

"My mission in life is not merely to survive, but to thrive; and to do so with some passion, some compassion, some humour, and some style."—Maya Angelou, poet

I love facial beauty masks. Most masks come infused with essential oils or soothing ingredients, which, when applied on the face, can deliver a high concentration that penetrates faster into the skin. Natural ingredients like yoghurt, papaya, or pineapple all have an exfoliating effect on the skin. Facial masks can give a smoothening or therapeutic effect for a temporary period of time, but typically do not last long. Whether a physical face mask or a psychological one, we have all hidden behind a mask at one time or the other. If you are reading this and not even admitting it, it could be a sign that you are currently hiding behind one.

Figuratively speaking, a "mask" is something you hide behind to present a different reality or an illusion far from what it is. Sometimes, you wear a mask placed on you by other people or circumstances without even realising it. Other times, you may deliberately wear one so you do not have to deal with the pressure, the pain, the surprise, the hurt, or even yourself in the light of an event, emotional turmoil, or when trying to show you are a strong woman who can cope with anything, when deep down inside, you know this is far from the truth.

When faced with tough times, the easier thing to do is to run and hide. When faced with our own realities, it's sometimes useful to recall the advice in the Gospel of Matthew, Chapter 7: "Remove the plank from your own eye, and then you will see clearly to remove the spec from your brother's eye."

When faced with tough times, the easier thing to do is to run and hide. When faced with our own realities, it's sometimes easier to blame the tiny speck in other people's eyes rather than remove the log of wood in our own.

Unfortunately, if you wear a mask long enough, it can sometimes get so comfortable that you forget who you really are, until someone comes along to help you see what you could become if you chose to stop hiding. A mask can be used to cover up nakedness and insecurity, almost the way flawless make-up covers the wrinkles and the spots on your face. A mask can be used as a shield of perfection when in reality, learning to embrace your flawed, vulnerable self is the surest way to freedom and joy.

I have worn a mask a few times. I was born after my parents already had three daughters. As I grew up and came to the realization that they had been hoping for a boy this time, I wore that mask for a while, trying to be the son my father yearned for. When puberty set in for most of my friends in high school, and they looked like beauty queens while here I was with short, kinky legs, I wore another mask in the form of long skirts because I thought my legs looked ugly. As a young wife, I wore a mask a few times, not asking for help or allowing myself to be pampered like a queen sometimes because I thought being the strong, independent woman my father raised meant not needing a man to complete her. I am so glad I changed that narrative – we've been happily married 22+ years and are still growing strong together.

I remember always cleaning and tidying up the house frantically lest anyone dropped by at any time to find a messy house. When you've got little kids running around the house, you know that it's impossible to maintain perfection. I learned to leverage help with childcare, housekeeping, grocery shopping, and even home massages, without feeling guilty. As I grew into my 30s, there were moments I cringed whenever my birthday was around the corner, simply because I didn't want to face the reality that I was "adulting", and life was getting serious now with taking care of the kids, managing dual careers, and increasing family responsibilities. Earlier in my career, I wore a few masks too. Finding myself as the only female or minority on an executive board or team sometimes made me feel not worthy of my accomplishments. When I met up with friends, I would consciously wear a mask to hide the privileges I enjoyed, or sometimes, be quiet or make myself small so I could fit into the "boys' club".

Many years ago, when I started my professional speaking career, I wore a mask a few times, saying yes to invitations I should have said no to, putting stress on my health when I knew I should be asleep in bed. The more I thought I was in control, the less in control I felt. Yet, on the outside, all people saw was my beaming unstoppable smile and can-do attitude. I wondered why people would call me only if they needed something. It baffled me why no one really gave towards my work or volunteered unless I asked. It took me a while to realize that on the outside I didn't look like someone who needed others. In my bid for perfection, I chased away potential helpers.

As a young career mum, I remember a time I was smashing goals on a project at work and everything was seemingly perfect, yet on the inside I judged myself harshly because my baby was not yet potty trained at an age most local mothers around me bragged about. I went to the office every day, masking that season of my life until I couldn't compartmentalize it anymore. One day, I sat in a private meeting room with my laptop open and sticky notes placed across the whiteboard with project timelines. If you peeped through the window, you would assume I was on the phone in a serious brainstorming session. Meanwhile, I did that just to look busy. Deep down, my heart was in pain, disappointed in my mothering skills. Not knowing what else to do, I looked up a senior colleague who I knew would have passed through this situation before when her kids were young. I called her and started by letting her know it was for a personal matter, not work related. She obliged and for the next half hour or more, I wiped the tears from my eyes as I explained to her what was going on with my mothering and asked for any tips she could give beyond the textbook advice the GP gave me.

As she listened and shared from her experiences, I could feel my inadequacies fading away. I was *not* a terrible mother excelling at work but terrible at home. I didn't have to pretend everything was okay. I could *give myself permission* to express my feelings and reach out for help or simply know that what I was experiencing was not unique to me and it was not a Best Mum contest. With patience and support, I freed myself from the "perfect mum" syndrome and have been free ever since. Looking back, that situation resolved itself when, one day, that kid got up, pulled off the nappies, walked away and repeated "no", or shook his head any time I tried to put the nappies back on.

Maybe you are reading this and saying: "That's not such a big deal." That's okay! Your mask may be different from mine. Like when things aren't going well in your relationships and someone asks: "How are you?", your default answer is "*amazing, great, awesome*", when the truth is you cry yourself to sleep every night! You post an amazing selfie on social media with the hashtag #livingthelife when your reality is far from it. Or you're worried about your finances but keep racking up your credit card bills from shopping online because you feel the need to be seen wearing the latest trends or always look good on the outside.

Maybe for you it is about living up to the pressure of what I call the "Big Auntie" syndrome, where you cannot let your guard down because your mentees are constantly watching. Or investing in yet another unhealthy slimming diet because you've got to get back your 20-year-old body, single chin, flat stomach, face free of wrinkles, because your self-esteem is anchored to that perfect body type. Maybe you are over 40, still single, and mask the fact that you are worried you might die alone. What is *your* mask? Take a moment to think about it.

Take the case of Isabella, an amazing business mogul who was in my coaching program. For a long time, Isabella sat on a fabulous business idea that could bring solutions to many people but remained in a university teaching job she found miserable, only because that was her parents' profession and their parents before them. But her heart often pulled her towards entrepreneurship. She would attend monthly family dinners at her parents' house pretending she was living the dream. Through our conversations, she found the courage to take off her mask of being the "good girl". Instead, she followed her dreams. In a little over a year, she was making a six-figure salary with that one idea.

Don't get me wrong. We don't necessarily have to spill out everything going on in our lives. There's some polishing and tweaking when we put things in context and on a need-to-know basis. However, the temptation to wear a mask is stronger if deep inside you feel you have to act or say things in a particular way to be loved and accepted.

Does this sound familiar? Exaggerating or bragging about your perfect weight, perfect life, perfect job, perfect family, adding extra bits to the conversation to portray a flourishing life? Yet, when the lights are out and the followers are gone, you look in the mirror and stare at the real you – wondering why you are unhappy and no one is offering help or support. The truth is, you never let them in because you worry they might find out you have been living a lie or half-truths. Being vulnerable is a sign of strength, and if you have real relationships in your life, you will find safety and security with those people and non-judgmental support as you unmask yourself.

Still wondering if you are really wearing a mask?

Here are five signs to check for:

1. You are a chronic people pleaser who craves being liked by others.
2. You fear criticism and would rather follow the crowd than make a different move.
3. You perpetually stay silent about what you really think and say something else.
4. Your worth is tied to other people's opinion of you.
5. You live in continual denial of reality, most times to your own detriment.

My challenge to you is this: How long will you tolerate the masked you when the real you is screaming for expression and fulfilment?

#2: Application Exercise: The Unveiling

List the top 5 roles you play in your life (personal and professional). How do these roles influence the masks you wear?

_____

_____

_____

When have you felt the need to wear a mask to fit societal expectations or avoid judgement?

_____

_____

_____

How to Unmask and Be Set Free

There's a television show called *The Masked Singer*[7], where celebrities dress in flamboyant costumes and masks and perform songs in front of an audience and a panel of judges. Each week, the audience votes for their favourite singer while the judges try to guess the identity of the personality behind the mask. As each week passes, a singer is unmasked, and the last singer standing is crowned the winner. You can almost feel the hearts throbbing each week as judges make guesses and gasp in amazement waiting to see who is behind

---

7 https://10play.com.au/the-masked-singer

the mask. The competition comes with loads of surprises and reveals the judges could never have imagined. In the end, no matter how hard the singers disguise themselves, the face behind the mask must be revealed.

In her research on the power of vulnerability, Brené Brown[8] describes vulnerability as the feeling of being unsure and uncertain in uncomfortable situations, especially when we are not sure how people will react to our vulnerability. She further explains that we can be scared and brave at the same time or confident and awkward at the same time, but we keep progressing anyway.

Take the case of one of my coaching clients, Grace, a senior executive in a top law firm and the only female on the executive board. Her impeccable track record, business acumen, and charisma always made her stand out in every role, and she had risen through the ranks in less than 10 years. Then, in her late 40s, Grace started experiencing perimenopausal symptoms that sometimes made her forget things or experience hormonal fluctuations. She knew something had to give. She loved her job and had a good CEO manager but, surrounded by men, it was difficult to explain why she would need a break every now and then from long meetings, or why she felt "hot" inside in a well air-conditioned room. One day, she had a conversation with her manager about what support and help looks like for her in this dream job of hers. "Fofo, it took guts to even bring up the subject," she said. "I felt our relationship was strong enough to handle it, and I am glad I eventually spoke up," Grace continued. Today, Grace still works for that company and has had more senior roles and global scope of responsibilities since then. Being vulnerable should not be perceived as a sign of weakness; rather, a

---

8 https://brenebrown.com/

behaviour of strength. Taking off our masks can bring positive relationships and connections into your life you never imagined.

Own Your Truth!

When I took off my masks one after the other, one of my new truths was "confident women ask for help". Another one was "I may not have all the answers yet, but I'll figure it out along the way." Own your truth. Define your truth. Get help in refining your truth. Let your awareness lead to productive action, fuelled by courage and renewed confidence. Share your new commitment with a trusted friend or supportive network who can hold you accountable. Also, write to me about your experience after going through this exercise. I respond to every letter or email I get. If you are also looking for a supportive community, consider joining the Flourishing 40s Collective at www.flourishingforties.com and make the most of this amazing decade of life.

#3: Application Exercise:
It's over to you now:

Think about a moment when you felt completely authentic and true to yourself. What was the situation and how did it make you feel?

_____

_____

Think of a time you chose vulnerability over wearing a mask and it led to a deeper connection or understanding? What did you learn from the experience?

_____

_____

In what area of your life might you still be wearing a mask?

_____

_____

What underlying beliefs or fears may be contributing to it?

_____

_____

Now that you are aware of it, challenging these beliefs, what is your new truth?

_____

_____

Lessons Learned

"I didn't come here to make sandwiches. I came to make business."
– Madam C. J. Walker, entrepreneur

I once took a few days off work for a staycation. I spent a big part of that time replenishing my spiritual, physical, and mental health. I also renewed my subscription to Netflix to watch a few movies. I stumbled on *Self Made*, a movie about Madam C. J. Walker (1867–1919). Born as Sarah Breedlove, the daughter of former slaves, Walker went from being an uneducated farm labourer and laundress to becoming the first female black millionaire in the United States and one of the twentieth century's most successful self-made female entrepreneurs. The movie producers took us behind the scenes – her struggles, her pain, her home, her business, and her life. Here are a few lessons I learned after I watched *Self Made*.

You do not have to motivate yourself to think negatively: The world is harsh enough. Look around you. Have you noticed miserable news sells faster and controversial videos go viral in milliseconds? It is so easy to think negative thoughts, to look around you and admire the seemingly greener grass in someone else's life, wishing it was your own. When life has dealt you lemons, it's easier to embrace the comfortable blanket of self-pity and stay in the valleys of the shadows of guilt, lack, intimidation, just feeling sorry for yourself.

It does not take much effort to feel small: Just the other day, my kids were playing hide-and-seek. The taller one crawled into a small space in a cupboard in the dining area while the other one scampered around the house looking for him. It took a few minutes to find his brother and by the time he was discovered, the taller one had cramp in his long legs from being squeezed into a small space. Seriously, it doesn't take any effort to feel small. All you have to do is roll yourself into a small ball in your mind and over-exaggerate the size of your threat or tormentor – that's it! As you age and face life's disappointments, it can be tempting to do just that. Do not let your circumstances win.

"No person is born great. Great people become great when others are sleeping." — African proverb

---

You do not have to dream: If you were not born with a silver spoon in your mouth and have never seen life outside your walls, you have a perfect excuse not to dream. However, the ability to dream is a universal and free gift. All you have to do is close your eyes. In no time, you can be transported to places, and see people or things that presently seem untouchable. We all have the natural ability to dream and that experience can be fuelled by a desire to reach for what is on the other side of your fears. Your dreams can also be constrained or enlarged by the environment around you and the kind of exposure you have with different people and cultures.

It all starts in the mind.

#4: Application Exercise: Who's Shaped Your Life:

Think of your life so far. Who are the top 3 people that have played a pivotal role in it?

    1. _____ (insert name)

The scenario

_____

_____

_____

A lesson I learned was:

_____

_____

_____

    2. _____ (insert name)

The scenario

_____

_____

_____

A lesson I learned was:

_____

_____

_____

3. _____ (insert name)

The scenario

_____

_____

_____

A lesson I learned was:

_____

_____

_____

As you close this chapter and refresh your decade, remember this moment. If you are tired of playing it safe, I invite you to adopt this mantra: *"I've got this one life to live and I have had enough of rekindling dead dreams."*

Be careful of the self-sabotaging stories you have told yourself until now and the labels culture or education have consciously or unconsciously given you to wear. A seed of greatness, when planted, yields fruits of greatness. Your driving force should be something bigger than you.

PART TWO
Summer: New Beginnings

Truth Sets Free

Here is a truth:
You cannot control everything.
In this truth is freedom and happiness.
An awakening to focus on what matters

There is another truth:
You were born for such a time as this.
What time is this, you may ask?
The time to flourish!

Celebrate your progress.
The strength that you possess
The opportunities you can still access
These truths will keep you in high places.

© Mofoluwaso Ilevbare

CHAPTER 4:
Now you're Adulting

"I am loving the woman I have grown into and am embracing the woman I am becoming." —Mofoluwaso Ilevbare

The year was 2019. Finally, I turned 40. I had a beautiful birthday party, and family and friends all glammed up in dinner gowns and suits. A few celebrities were invited as speakers. I also organized a mini conference during the birthday celebration with motivational strategies from the keynote speaker and panellists about flourishing in our 40s. As the months went by, I started to notice some interesting things that I hadn't paid much attention to earlier. Here are some of them:

- My metabolism and ability to digest certain kinds of food became slower.
- Going out after 8p.m. started to feel like an expensive sacrifice.
- Non-sugary drinks actually taste good.
- My inner circle of friends is growing smaller.

- My first strands of grey/white hair began to spring up in some weird places.

- I have an urgency to make a more meaningful impact with my life.

- The more time I spend living my values and prioritizing what matters most in this season, the more resolute I am becoming.

- Some things that seemed so important before do not bother me anymore.

- My kids love cooking meals, and I rarely have to now.

- I rarely feel FOMO (Fear of Missing Out). If I cannot be there, so be it. Oh, the bliss…

- Goodbye high heels… welcome, comfy shoes! Where have you been my entire life?

- No matter how much I wish for it, nothing changes until I get up and do.

Fresh Starts May Be Uncomfortable

In my career, I have had the rare privilege of moving to new countries and collaborating with diverse teams across the whole of Africa, India, the Middle East, Europe, United States, Asia, Australia and New Zealand. I have experienced visiting colleagues, sometimes working and living in beautiful cities like Brussels, Casablanca, Alexandria, Dubai, Cairo, Johannesburg, Sydney, Geneva, Cincinnati, Istanbul, Atlanta, St. Petersburg, Mumbai, Auckland… the list goes on and on. I have been privileged to speak on many stages in front of complete strangers and many times as a minority speaker. I have witnessed countless personal and organizational transformations of leaders and students in my coaching programs and consulted for various companies and small to medium-sized enterprises.

As my career progressed, I relocated thrice alone, and thrice with my husband and kids. In one of those roles, around 2005–2006, I joined a project team on a mission to a sister company in Cairo, where we would live for almost a year developing people capability, systems, and infrastructure, as we needed to build a detergent manufacturing plant and organisation from scratch. The moment I got on the plane, I noticed the change in culture – the way of speaking and mode of dressing. From the airport, we were transported by bus to our new home. On the way, I remember looking through the window with curiosity, admiring the sandy horizons and desert view, hoping that this adventure would turn out well, just like the others.

Between 2010–2011, I relocated to Belgium on another career growth experience, which happened to coincide with one of the harshest winter seasons the world had experienced. I remember being stuck at the airport once or twice, not being able to fly back home as often to see my family, and sometimes feeling alone and deserted in my cold white-walled, two-bedroom apartment. Two months into that work assignment, I was surprised to find out that I was pregnant. The news was unexpected considering we had waited about five years to have our first baby. The doctor classified me as a delicate case and instructed that I go on immediate bed rest until the first trimester was over. Alas, I had been away from my home country for a few weeks and missed my family. I also wanted to break the news to my husband face to face. Despite the doctor's orders to maintain strict bed rest for a while, I secretly booked a weekend return ticket and boarded a plane to see my family. The flight home was a turbulent one, and the trip was stressful. Somehow, due to my heightened stress and blood pressure level, I lost the pregnancy. I was inconsolable. Getting pregnant again without any medical intervention was a miracle I wished had stayed. I blamed myself for months for being stubborn and making such a grave mistake. Eventually, I forgave myself and released the pain, thanks to my faith, a supportive counsellor, and a strong family support system.

Still on fresh starts, a few weeks after my fortieth birthday, my family had to embark on our fifth international relocation, this time to Australia. Three months after our relocation, the world went into lockdown due to the rapid spread of the COVID-19 virus. Relocating to a new culture, city, or country can be exciting but also scary and uncomfortable. Doing so at a time of a global uncertainty and crisis was even more unnerving. Finding people to trust, learning new ways of living, learning to drive on the opposite side of the road, and sometimes pivoting into a new career path proved daunting. Can you relate?

Looking back, I cherish the remarkable opportunities and experiences my family has had travelling across continents, exploring new languages, experiencing new cultures, making community impact, and trying out new food. But one common downside we experienced was not having enough time to develop and nurture new relationships before we had to move again. For that reason, for me, *home is not where the heart is; home is where my immediate family is,* because I have a piece of *my heart (family, friends, and even some luggage)* in different places across the world.

Fresh Starts and Summertime

Summertime is usually a fun time when kids are mostly on holidays (depending on which part of the world and the school curriculum). Summertime gives families the chance to relax and travel together. In our 40s season, summertime can metaphorically mean a fresh start, new beginnings, new work, new love, new opportunities, laughter at dinner tables, bright focus and vision, loving your body more, making new friends, finding your dream job and career, and all things bright and beautiful. However, summertime can also bring with it some sweat, stickiness, and hot temperatures. Life has a way of throwing curveballs that can force you into a halt that catapults a fresh start, and sometimes this may happen when you are least expecting it.

Reflecting on the Bridges Transition Model[9] we discussed earlier, life can bring with it some endings, a neutral zone, or a new beginnings zones. Your level of self-awareness and ability to realign your life will determine the speed and quality of your transition through the zones.

> Recognize (the change) → Review (who or what needs to change) → Respond (when and how).

A fresh start can be like a breath of fresh air, an opportunity to harness an untapped potential or territory. A fresh start can also feel like a tornado, unsettling everything you have built to support you, giving you little or no control. Not everyone loves a fresh start, especially one you did not choose yourself. But it could be the best thing ever to happen to you, and your attitude towards that season can determine how successful, happy, healthy, or wealthy you can be.

---

9 https://wmbridges.com/about/what-is-transition/

The months of isolation due to the forced COVID-19 lockdowns in Australia, working from home, changing jobs in between, shuttling incessantly between working from my home office and homeschooling the kids was for me a "roller-coaster" season but also perfect timing to lean on each other as a family and fortify our values.

False Start to Fresh Start

I am a fan of Usain Bolt, the Jamaican-born athlete, eight-time Olympic gold medallist and, at the time of writing this book, the world record holder in the 100m, 200m, and 4x100m relay competitions. I witnessed one of the horror moments of his career: a false start – and subsequent disqualification – during the 2011 World Championships in Korea. He was undoubtedly the favourite to win that race and defend his title, but it was not meant to be. When interviewed by the *New York Times*, he said:

"Of course I am extremely disappointed not to have had the chance to defend my title due to the false start. I was feeling great through the rounds and was ready to run fast in the final. I worked very hard to get ready for this championship, and things were looking good. However, I have to move on now, as there is no point to dwell on the past."[10]

What a great mindset! Usain Bolt bounced back from that incident and went on to win many more medals and titles before officially retiring in 2017. He continues to support aspiring athletes and make an impact.

---

10 https://www.nytimes.com/2011/08/30/sports/30iht-arena30.html

When I look around me, the new crop of forticians (women over 40) are adulting differently. They are looking fabulous, smashing goals, building empires, venturing more and more into male-dominated sectors, and trying new things. Women are more conscious of their health, planning well, and making an impact.

A tree that doesn't bloom in its season can be disappointing. When a tree blooms in its season, we all enjoy the richness of its fruits and the beauty of fresh flowers. This season, I am inviting you to join the forest of forticians who are trailblazing their 40s with a fresh start. Learn more at www.flourishingforties.com.

Fresh Start: The 5 Ds to Consider

1. **Discovery**: Ask yourself: "Who am I, really? Where am I now?" This is the starting point. The ability to recognise who you are and the path you are on is the catalyst to flourishing in your 40s.

2. **Destination:** "Where am I going? What do I want to do by the time I turn 50?" Most modern cars have a GPS installed to help with navigation. When you input an address, the GPS creates route options to help you get there. Even with the best GPS system, without an input, there is no output.

3. **Determination:** "How will I evolve so that I get there from here?" Nothing changes until you take steps to bring things into reality. What will you stand for? What would you fight for? What could get in your way, and how will you manage distractions?

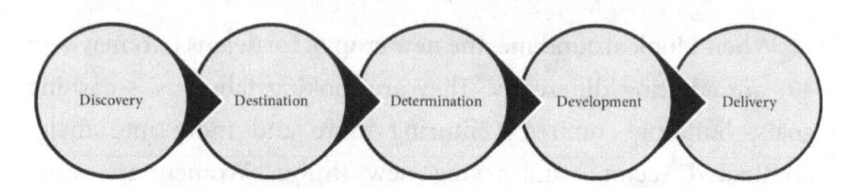

Discovery → Destination → Determination → Development → Delivery

4. **Development:** "What capabilities do I need? By when?" What skills will propel you forward? Place a demand on yourself to be more knowledgeable, influential, and impactful in this season.

5. **Delivery:** "What support systems will power up my journey?" Who could you ask to support you, and what do you need them to do for you? Recognise the resources you will need – the right systems, habits, people, positioning, and platforms.

#5 Application Exercise: F.R.E.S.H. Start

Instructions: Choose the closest answer:

1. **When I am faced with uncertainty, I:**

a) Embrace it as an opportunity.

b) Feel a bit uneasy but adapt eventually.

c) Prefer what is familiar and struggle with change.

2. **My approach to learning new skills is to:**

a) Actively seek opportunities.

b) Adapt when necessary but not always proactively.

c) Stick to what I already know.

3. **When confronted with setbacks, I:**

a) See them as opportunities for growth.

b) Experience initial frustration but adapt over time.

c) Struggle to bounce back from setbacks.

4. **When a fresh start triggers life transitions, I:**

a) Actively embrace and navigate life transitions with resilience.

b) Tend to navigate transitions, but with some emotional challenge.

c) Struggle to embrace life transitions, and often feel overwhelmed.

Were your answers mostly a, b, or c?

- Mostly a's: Fantastic! Your flexibility to adapt and openness to change is your superpower. Keep embracing this mindset and keep learning.

- Mostly b's: It is great you are open to change even if it takes a while. Reflect on your progress and keep taking small meaningful steps.

- Mostly c's: I get it! Change can be challenging. Think about why you feel some resistance and get support to shift your perspectives without being overwhelmed.

How else can you ensure your fresh start is not a false start? You can start by applying the F.R.E.S.H. tips (Freshen, Reprioritize, Evolve, Systemize, and Hope).

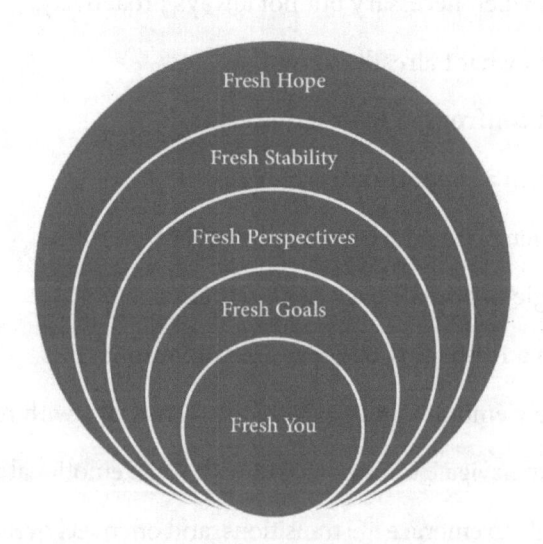

- Fresh Hope
- Fresh Stability
- Fresh Perspectives
- Fresh Goals
- Fresh You

- **Freshen Up:** I term this as a **Fresh You.** Take a good look in the mirror. Do you love, I mean really looooove, who and what you see? Do you feel fresh on the outside as well as the inside? Take a moment and process that thought. What aspect of your life can you freshen up to celebrate this season of life? It does not necessarily mean acting completely out of character, squandering your life's savings or packing a backpack and heading off to climb Everest. Some simple areas to get you started could be a) your closet, b) your hair, c) your schedules, d) your professional or social circle, e) your make-up bag, f) your speaking or confidence, g) your LinkedIn bio or resume, h) your exercise routine, g) your quiet/meditation periods, h) your eating habits, i) the time you spend with your spouse / family.

- **Reprioritise:** Let's call this **Fresh Goals:** While some suggest declaring January 17 as "Ditch Your New Year's Resolution Day,"[11] other research suggests setting goals that reach for something rather than avoiding something.[12] I recommend setting intentions instead and reviewing them every 90 days. For example, last year, instead of setting new goals, I simply went over my vision board and highlighted five areas where I have been procrastinating. My intentional phrase for the year was "Finish what you started!" Three goals stood out for me: completing my doctoral research, joining a fitness accountability group, and working on this book project/related tasks so I can help more forticians flourish in their 40s. I accomplished all three! When you assess and

---

11 Ditch New Year's Resolutions Day, January 17 Holiday. (holidayinsights.com)
12 A large-scale experiment on New Year's resolutions: Approach-oriented goals are more successful than avoidance-oriented goals - PMC (nih.gov)

redefine your priorities, you stand a better chance of being a starter and a finisher.

- **Evolve:** Whether it's running a business, learning or re-learning a skill, becoming a first-time mum, pivoting your career, starting a new business, or rediscovering your purpose, commit yourself to something significant. American executive coach Marshall Goldsmith wrote a book called *What Got You Here Won't Get You There*, a concept that aligns with the second metric of the Adaptability Quotient: learnability. See change as a challenge, a catalyst for growth. Your brain can adapt. Be bold. Embrace new beginnings. I call this **Fresh Perspectives.**

- **Systemize:** Do you currently have systems that keep you grounded, steady, and consistent? Do your habits support your goals?[13] In this decade, you will need to establish new boundaries and solidify new networks that help you flourish in our unpredictable world. I call this **Fresh Stability.** Like a ship steady through a storm, the right systems will keep you grounded, organized, and unshaken.

- **Hope:** Hope is not just a state of mind. It is an active force that drives us to set goals and achieve them. People who are hopeful tend to experience better health, better psychological and social well-being, and lower levels of stress-induced outcomes.[14] When you approach your 40s with **Fresh Hope**, you become more optimistic and unstoppable.

---

[13] Habits and Goals in Human Behavior: Separate but Interacting Systems - Wendy Wood, Asaf Mazar, David T. Neal, 2022 (sagepub.com)
[14] The role of Hope in subsequent health and well-being for older adults: An outcome-wide longitudinal approach - ScienceDirect

Chapter 5:
Purpose and Vision

"The most pathetic person in the world is someone who has sight but has no vision."
–Helen Keller, disability rights advocate

Last weekend, my ten year old drew a picture of a gigantic noodle shop he hopes to own in the future. You can guess that his favourite food at this point in his life is noodles. He's an enthusiastic junior chef who makes his own noodles and egg, trying out different recipes and various ways of cooking it every time. In addition to that, he mentioned he wants to be a mathematician, a YouTube video gamer, and even a Hungry Jack's attendant (so that he gets to serve others at the drive-by and eat a free chicken burger every day). When kids talk about the future, they paint incredibly inspiring pictures for us of being an astronaut, a medical doctor, or something close. These dreams might seem unachievable to us as adults, but to them, there are no limits. They are not worried about cost, or consequences, and see their parents as superheroes who can make anything happen.

Somewhere along the line, the "adulting" process begins. Education, environment, social and emotional experiences, and changes in life start to reshape their thinking and sometimes stunt those ideas. In the "adulting" process, big dreams can get watered down by the negative things we experience, what people say, the stories we tell ourselves. Before we know it, we are settling for less, comfortable with safe, or making up stories and theories we want to believe. On the other hand, becoming an adult gives us an opportunity to be in the driver's seat of our life and author our own story.

When you hold a seed in your hand, what is the first thing that comes to mind? You see the plain seed as simply a seed, which is the way we sometimes perceive our lives too. You most likely don't envision a tree with big juicy mangoes or big flabby branches where birds chirp sweetly every morning, with a wooden bench placed under the tree to provide shade for anyone who sits there. When an experienced farmer plants a seed, they envision how big it could grow and the potential harvest yield.

Imagining a better world or something extraordinary is possible through the power of vision. Vision is a picture of what is possible beyond the reality of your present circumstances. We all have the capacity to dream but not everyone responds to their dreams. Do you see yourself accomplishing your dreams? Do you see yourself in your 40s as healthier, functional, free, wealthy, and whole, or do you see yourself lonely, depressed, dying alone, stuck in a job you hate, with no friend in the world?

"The greatest tragedy in life is not death, but a life without purpose."
–Myles Munroe

Think about the tons of pictures you have in your phone photo gallery. I bet not all of them qualify to be posted on the internet. Most of us edit our pictures before we post online. I know I do. For a few minutes, I review the pictures, delete if my arms look too big or my belly too wide or my face looks funny. You know what I'm referring to. We mostly post photos we feel good about. Now, think about the pictures (vision) of your life that you capture in your mind every day. What type of pictures and thoughts about your life are you creating every day? Do they reflect your values and the positive dreams of a life you truly love?

For example, for me, marriage and family is a big part of who I am. Since I discovered the power of vision boards, I've created one for my family and review it every year. I remember a particular year in South Africa where, after three days of learning indoors, we decided to enjoy the sunshine in Cape Town. This was a trip with a difference. I not only got to attend the event with my husband, but we were also able to take the kids as well. My vision board had a picture of a family vacation in South Africa, but with no pre-planned vacation fund and no relatives in that country at that time, how in the world could this dream manifest?

I pinned that vision board to a wall in the bedroom and prayed over it every morning. Somewhere within the first quarter of the year, a leadership training event popped up with highly subsidized fees for couples who would attend and live on the grounds. My husband Joshua and I saw it, and we felt it was a good investment for both our professional careers, so we jumped on a discovery call to learn more about it. When we were satisfied it was a chance not to miss, the question was "where do we keep the kids?" We searched Facebook to find any friends or past acquaintances who might be living in South Africa and asked for ideas. Through a friend, we found a post-graduate student who doubled as a nanny. We interviewed her virtually (this was way before Zoom) and agreed to hire her. We found a lovely self-serviced apartment online that had a good family package and got on the plane, with a 75% discount on all our expenses. While Joshua and I attended the events during the day, the guest-house manager, and the nanny (she was God-sent) ensured the kids had a great time. In the evenings, we had family time, and over the weekend visited monumental places in Cape Town: we saw Nelson Mandela's cell at Robben Island, Seal Island, and the Twelve Apostles mountains along the Atlantic coast of Cape Town, and enjoyed watching various groups perform the indigenous dances.

What were the odds of this happening that year, that fast, with 75% of our expenses paid for? Whether it is framed on a physical board, a digital process, or a plan, the vision you can see is a powerful thing. When you have an unobstructed vision, you become a potential agent of change. An inspiring vision can disrupt your internal thought process and drive you to action till what you see on the inside matches what you see on the outside. That is the power of visioning.

Benefits of Having a Vision

Vision drives purpose. Standing close to the prison cell of the late Nelson Mandela, I could not fathom how a human being could endure 27 years in the harsh conditions of that tiny space without losing his mind and his tenacious commitment to freedom and equality. His time behind bars solidified his resolve to end apartheid and build a South Africa rooted in justice and inclusivity. Upon his release, Mandela's forgiveness and reconciliation efforts set the stage for a new era, proving that change could be achieved without hatred or revenge. Want to find your purpose? Your purpose already is inside you. Create a strong vision, and it will fuel your purpose. And when you step into your purpose, you give others the permission to be inspired by your story and do the same.

It is not wishful thinking: A visionary mindset can be described as "a conscious understanding of the power of your mind's eye to see what is not visible to the naked eye and [the ability to] make it happen". To envision requires leaning into a future that does not yet exist and bringing it to reality. Like a compass guiding your life, your vision coordinates is where you return whenever you get confused about anything in your life, work, and relationships.

"Success is not to be pursued; it is to be attracted by the person you become" –Jim Rohn

Attracts provision: From people to places to profits to possibilities, when you have a clear vision, you will engage the right people, actions, and goals to bring it to pass. A clear vision can make you wealthy – not just in terms of your bank account, but wealthy in time, resources, relationships, invention, and ideas. A wealthy woman breeds a wealthy nation. A wealthy woman can sponsor others. A wealthy woman is the pride of her community, family, and the nation. Wealth opens doors. Wealth answers prayers and needs. Wealth removes barriers. Wealth gives you a seat at certain tables. Get wisdom and get wealth. A clear vision gives you access to both.

Sharpens your focus: Have you ever thought to yourself "I want to buy a white 4WD Tesla." The moment you think it, your mind's eye goes to work. You start to imagine yourself in one. As you drive through traffic, at the mall, at the gym, you start to see the brand pop up everywhere. It is called the *red car syndrome*. You may overhear someone talking about it or catch an ad on TV. What changed? Clarity brings your vision into focus and every other thing that does not look like what you imagine becomes a distraction.

Builds your confidence: I love to watch budding entrepreneurs make their pitches on the TV program "Shark Tank". You can tell which entrepreneur is confident about their products and prospects as the sharks challenge their thinking. Confidence is like a muscle. We can grow more confident. The more confident you are, the more likely you are to project your vision and influence others. It embodies what you think, feel, see, hear and do.

Challenges the norm: There are many stereotyped societal norms we've been raised to believe and accept. A clear vision may smash your beliefs and challenge status quo. Have you noticed that athletes we rave about set previously unimaginable records? This would not have been possible if they had stayed on script. A well-thought-out vision is innovative, revolutionary, and forward-thinking.

Keeps you energised: Motivational gurus tell us that rich people don't sleep or that they start their day from 5 am. I interpret this differently. When you are driven by a vision, sometimes you may lose sleep over it. You have a waking thought, and you feel a rush of energy to do something about it. It doesn't mean you shouldn't sleep or if you wake up at 5 am daily, you automatically become rich. Sleep is a proven source of renewable energy. If you've ever been driven by a vision, in the midst of pain or discomfort you experience an inner push to press on, against all odds.

Helps you fish beyond your postcode: You've probably heard it over and over again that you are a product of your environment. Caveat: do not let your environment cloud your future. Harness the power of the internet and globalize your mind, spirit and body. Diversify your visionary portfolio, your belief system, your investments, and your digital impact footprints. Your great grandchildren will thank you, and if you have no kids, the lives you touch would remember your name.

Ignites transformation: Whenever Apple or Samsung announce the launch of a new phone, I think to myself, "What could possibly be different about this new model and the one in my hand?" To TRANSFORM your life, TRANS-late the good knowledge you've already acquired into an actionable FORM that upgrades your capacity (inborn ability), capability (acquired ability), and credibility (trust credit with others).

Activates speed: You experience a restlessness to achieve something. When you have a vision, you spend your time and resources more wisely. We waste so much time, energy, and resources on the wrong things. Check your life bank account. How much time do you waste on liabilities or energy drainers? How much money did you invest in fruitless pursuits? How many times did you talk yourself out of hard work because it was not trending? A clear vision activates speed to do what matters most.

Controls your talk: A clear vision takes centrepiece in your mind. It releases you from unnecessary and mindless chatter. You are mindful of how you speak, to whom, and what you say. You won't burn bridges anyhow because you know where you are heading and how your integrity or brand should be protected. You won't share your vision with small-minded people who could destroy your creativity or enthusiasm to pursue. A clear vision coupled with a disciplined life will help you start and finish well.

Is victorious: Creating a compelling vision for your life or career does not mean things will always automatically fall in place. Visionary leaders see themselves as victors, not victims. Actualising your dream will cost you. To accomplish your goals, foster a victor's mentality. A clearer vision can help you leverage the power of *yet*. I am not good at this *yet*, but I will do x, y, or z to get better. This is a concept Carol Dwerk enlightens us with in her book, *Mindset: The New Psychology of Success*. She differentiates a fixed mindset and a growth mindset. A visionary person evolves and grows with a growth mindset.

Supports something bigger than you: A vision board is a personal vision of your desires. However, a vision board can be selfish – filled with pictures and dreams of wants, not the needs that can make our world a better place. As you progress in your 40s, don't be selfish. A woman of virtue has a vision which never benefits her alone, but everyone else around her. The same way a tree freely gives its beautiful leaves, fruits, and branches for shade, you must remember you are made for more.

Produces a fruitful and healthy life: Everything takes its perfect form when the time is ripe. Take the orange, for instance. An orange contains citric acid, which is good for the body. But the same orange could be poisonous if it is eaten unripe. When you plant a good seed, you expect a good harvest. What do you envision as you think about the next decade of your life? How well will you plan ahead so you can live a fruitful and healthy life? Your imagination dictates your actions. Your imagination will pull you towards the life you dream of.

#6 Application Exercise: Check-In

Think about your personal vision:

What is your personal vision, now that you are in your 40s? How clearly have you defined it?

_____

_____

How connected do you feel right now to your purpose and personal vision?

_____

_____

If there is a misalignment, what adjustments can you make to get back on track?

_____

_____

What are your top 5 core values, and how are they serving you in becoming a better person?

_____

_____

CHAPTER 6:
Charting Your Path

"A blurry vision is like having eyes that work but a mind that's blind to possibilities."
–Mofoluwaso Ilevbare

Once we were on a much-anticipated family trip to the countryside, eager to spend quality time together. We made several stops along the way, soaking in iconic views and visiting tourist attractions. As we approached the village where we planned to spend the night, the weather changed and we suddenly found ourselves driving through a thick, misty fog. My husband, who was driving, found his vision becoming increasingly blurry. He started relying on his instincts. He switched on the fog lights *and* the hazard lights while the heated windscreen wipers worked tirelessly to help us see what was ahead.

Have you ever driven a car in the rain with no wipers? It is risky, isn't it? We finally reached our destination and enjoyed a safe and enjoyable weekend. Think about your vision for your life and this decade. Is your vision blurry right now? Have the circumstances of your past dimmed your light? Get your wipers out. Switch on your headlights. If you wear glasses, I bet you clean the lenses regularly to have a clearer vision. Life demands the same response.

Capture the Vision

When I was in primary school, we were forced to practise quiet times, during which the teacher would tell us to put our heads on the table and rest. Or else we would have "time out" – moments when we had to sit in a naughty corner, calm down, and think about what we had done. It is interesting that as you become an adult, no one forces you to have "thinking time", times of sober reflection, times to imagine a world bigger than our circumstances, and many of us don't intentionally include those quiet times into our schedule anymore. You must be deliberate about creating such times.

Our deepest awakening takes place in the "spaces" of our lives. The more you practice, the better you become at conscious thinking. It is beyond mere mindfulness or meditation. It is a deliberate attempt to quiet the noise around you so you can really see what's ahead.

So, close your eyes for another minute or two.

Whose vision are you following?

Your vision is a reflection of who you are or want to be. If your vision is not yours, it will not last, or it will bring strain into your life. Imagine your health improving. Imagine your business growing despite economic inflation. Imagine a loving marriage. Imagine your children doing well. Imagine your soul being refreshed and free. Can you see it? Can you see yourself beyond today, from local to global, flourishing and growing from being a seed to a mighty cedar or oak tree? Capture what you see.

Have a renewed vision and new goals. Paint a picture of your future that will keep you running. Don't let the past distort your new vision. Your vision will evolve over time. As you grow and catch another glimpse of the future, you retouch the plans. You may not have a full clear picture of the entire journey. Sometimes, the ideas that drop into your mind are glimpses and tiny pieces of the puzzle. As an idea comes into your mind, take action before your brain starts to rationalise and smother the idea. Ideas bring creativity. Your vision governs your world. You will find movement and fulfilment as you move forward.

Document the vision

Documenting your vision is a form of life crafting, the process of consciously reviewing all important aspects of your life and creating a plan congruent with your values. There is a direct relationship between having a purpose in life and a decrease in mortality, mental health problems, anxiety, and many other related conditions.[15] When you have a clear purpose in life, you are more likely to make better decisions related to health, wealth, and impact.

Get a piece of paper or journal and write down 10 things you want to accomplish before you turn 50. Imagine there are no limitations and just write. Document that vision in the form of an audio, video, words, or a combination of the three, so you don't forget it. Use whatever means necessary to keep your vision in view year after year. It might be a vision book, a vision board, a vision reel, or a podcast. It won't be perfect when you start, but the vision gets clearer, the weight starts shedding, your customers start growing,

---

15 https://doi.org/10.3389/fpsyg.2019.02778

your faith and confidence rise. Challenge what is not working in your life right now. Face it with boldness and take charge of your next steps. Tell yourself *"I'd rather fail and learn and grow than wake up at 80 and wish I had taken the first step."* A spark of a matchstick can set a forest or a house on fire.

A powerful vision comes with a deep conviction that you were born to do something significant, and this does not have to be feeding one billion people on the planet or inventing something that outlasts generations. *Your* vision ignites purposeful work, which could be within a local, global, or virtual community. If you want to learn more about how to create a strong vision for your life, check my website for some resources.

Activate the Vision

A few years ago, immediately after Easter, I went to a designer store offering some ridiculous sales, knowing I could get a 30% discount on whatever I bought that day. I had seen the advert on a friend's timeline, and I wanted to cash in on it. My eyes moved to and fro through the store until I found this fabulous zebra-striped jacket. I knew it would fit perfectly with my new pair of pink pants. I quickly grabbed my size (it was the last one), turned left to the changing room area and tried it on. It fit perfectly. Woohoo!! My day was made already. I rushed to the cashier to pay for it. The cashier kept punching in the code and fiddling around with the keyboard mouse.

Then she looked up at me and said, "I'm sorry, ma'am. This jacket is not on sale." "Oh no!" I exclaimed. I stared at the jacket a little while longer. I could visualize myself wearing it together with my pair of pink pants while attending a leadership conference gig the following week. I thought about it for a while trying to see which impulse was stronger. *To buy or not to buy?* It's similar to hitting a hurdle while pursuing your dream. The differentiator in this case would be if your dream is more important. In that particular situation, my hopes and vision were dashed. I probed further as to why the jacket was not on sale and what would need to be true to take it home with me. After consulting with the business owner, I paid a few more bucks and walked out with my beautiful find – to me, it was worth it.

Stop negotiating with yourself or your dream. Go after your dream. Pursue it. Every great dream has a cost attached to it. Are you willing to pay the price? There is no "perfect" time to live your dreams and implement your vision. *Start right now*! If there were no limitations, what would you aspire to achieve? When you become a fortician, you put away childish things. If you are still hung up about trivial things, it's time to get serious with your life. Make a plan and create structures and systems to implement your plan and review them periodically. Dream up images that connote words like freedom, empowerment, flourish, fruitful, abundance, healthy, energized. What relationships do you need to build?

I once had a client, Roseline, who struggled with sticking to a healthy lifestyle. Her excuses kept getting in her way. With guided coaching, she took steps to replace the images her mind's eye was focusing on. She picked "healthy" as her word of the year, and she envisioned what her life could look like if it was a healthy one. Then, she splashed her intentions and actions on sticky notes and her Google calendar, cleaned out her fridge with the word "healthy" in mind, reviewed her credit card payments and what she spent money on, and checked her schedules to review how many times she ate out and the people/habits that set her back every time she had a little win. With discipline and small steps, she made the big shift in her life and is still going.

Pass on the Vision

I love watching the 4x100m relay races at the Olympic Games. The very best four runners from the top countries in the world are competing for the gold medal. As the top athletes stretch and prepare for the race, the determinants are faultless starts, seamless baton exchanges, speed in their strides, and teamwork. The noise of the starting gun triggers the opening leg, which sets the tone for what is to come. As the last exchange is made, you can feel the tension in the stadium, all eyes on the last leg till they cross the finish line. Each team member must trust the other and hand off the baton purposefully till they accomplish the vision in their minds – the pride that comes with the gold medal around their neck and the tune of their national anthem beating in their souls.

Passing the baton can be likened to the moment the tree drops its fruits, or sheds its leaves or its seeds to the ground. Every seed represents a vision passed from one generation to another. When a seed is nurtured in good soil, it germinates and sprouts, breaking through the limitations called life. As the trunk gives it stability and height, the branches extend and expand, taking up space and making an impact. When seeds find good soil and grow into new trees, the vision is multiplied until the environment becomes a forest, a collective effort.

If your vision is all about what you can have, where you can live, how much money you want to make, then I challenge you to think bigger. Your vision gives meaning and direction to your life. It should be the catalyst and motivation for all that you do – the *why* that pulls you out of bed. It should also be contagious and influence others to change their behaviour or perspective because you helped them "see" the unseeable and have the audacity to think the impossible.

Your vision should outlast you!

#7 Application:
Vision Unleashed

How do you measure progress or success in achieving your vision and goals?

_____

_____

_____

What resources and visual aids can you use to enhance your personal vision?

_____

_____

_____

When you find yourself losing sight of your goals, what strategies would you use to regain clarity and direction?

_____

_____

_____

If you are unsure of your path forward, what next step can you take right now?

_____

_____

_____

In the next 10 years, what do you see yourself doing with the baton of life in your hand?

_____

_____

_____

CHAPTER 7:
The Big Aunties –Now I'm One of Them

"You can be gorgeous at 30, charming at 40, and irresistible for the rest of your life."
—Coco Chanel, fashion designer

Over the years, I have been privileged to speak to both high school and university students across the world. One of my recent initiatives was a virtual personal development/mentoring program that reached more than 2,000 university students across Africa who were stuck at home during the COVID-19 forced lockdowns. We called the project "Campus Ginger". We engaged several professors, experts, successful business owners, and international mentors to mentor the students in areas of leadership, career growth, and personal development. Before then, I remember being invited to a university campus to speak to the graduating class of engineering students about career development and finding your purpose in life. From the moment I stepped out of the car till I got back into the car, one phrase seemed to strike a nerve every time I heard it. It came out in various expressions like these…

"Hey, Big Auntie! Long time no see!" one said.

"Hey, Big Auntie… you are finally here," another echoed

"Auntie, we've been expecting you."

"Ma, I have a question."

"So, Big Auntie, when are you coming back to visit us?"

Note: The word "Aunt" or "Auntie" is used to describe the sister of your father or mother and the wife of your uncle; it can also be used informally to address an older woman or female adult.

Hearing the word made me cringe.

"Call me Fofo," I found myself repeating over and over again, but it seemed to fall on deaf ears. When did I become the "Auntie", I wondered. After my keynote, I sat back to enjoy the networking session and the rest of the conference. The more I looked around and listened to the conversations, the slang they used, and the gestures they displayed, the more I realized this was a bunch of people in a different season of life. In their own season, I was the big Auntie. On the one hand, I could choose to cringe when addressed as the "Big Auntie," or I could embrace the dignity and honourable role I was now elevated to where I had the opportunity to shape the lives of others while also living my best life.

Are you a millennial who just clocked 40 or a Gen X who is further along in your 40s? Welcome to the era of becoming a Big Auntie. Sometimes, when we use the term "millennial", we forget life isn't stagnant for this age group. Millennials are definitely growing older, and so are Gen Zs and every baby born since then. Like Catherine Shoichet wrote in a CNN column and I quote: *"The generation long portrayed as young and naïve is entering middle age."*[16]

One minute it seems like you were just in high school…the next minute you have become the big sister, mother, the carer, the boss lady, or the big Auntie.

- Where did the time go?
- Maybe your body can feel it – maybe your heart feels it, too.
- Maybe the responsibilities you now juggle are telling you the same thing.

"Life flourishes in the embrace of 'and,' not the constraints of 'either/or." – Mofoluwaso Ilevbare

---

It is ok to be the Big Auntie! Many of us in our 40s are juggling a career or business and the organisational politics that comes with it. Some of us are having kids and trying to keep up with childcare costs, managing ageing parents or siblings, paying mortgages, running a mogul empire, and trying to keep up with social trends and new ways of working. Some of us are single and happy, single and searching, or single and fed up. Some of us have found our rhythm; some of us are still trying to figure out what the heck life is really all about. We are in the prime of our lives and sometimes it feels like a thrill; other times, it's a rollercoaster of emotions. Going to the doctor for your annual check-ups was never a question, but

---

16 https://edition.cnn.com/2022/12/31/us/millennials-turning-40-shoichet-cec/index.html

maybe now you go with your heart beating with the hope you leave with a clean bill of health. You look around you, and just like that, it seems you are no longer the life of the party – you may have become the Big Auntie.

What do you do when you realise you are now the Big Auntie?

Appreciate life: Ageing is a gift. It simply means you are alive and still have a chance to enjoy the vigour and vitality that anyone six feet under right now would beg for. I love it when I read incredible stories of people in their 70s, 80s, and even 90s, still enjoying life and making a significant impact. It is a new way of thinking and living. Who decides what your life should be like in your 40s? You! Start with what you are grateful for. Make a list. Then assess how well you are maximizing your seasons – are you seeding, rooting, growing, blooming, or renewing?

Embrace your new chapter and do not be defined by titles: Whether Gen X, Millennial, Big Auntie, or whatever, acknowledge the shift but do not be defined by the generalisations. Tell yourself, "My age, job title, or bank account balance do not define me." This truth will free you from societal pressure or lack of. In this new season, you have permission to break the rules and write new ones. Look around you – Big Aunties are having a ball! How can you continue to create value and enjoy life, comfortable in your own skin?

Honour your body: This bodily suit you are wearing right now needs to be nurtured and cared for. So does your mind. What will make a difference 40 years from now depends on the actions you take today. In a speech he gave to a group of college students at Omaha,

Nebraska, American investor and philanthropist Warren Buffet said, "*You only get one mind and you only get one body. And it's got to last a lifetime... If you don't take care of that mind and that body, they'll be a wreck 40 years later.*"[17]. What habits do you practise to honour your body? Be consistent and kind to yourself.

Manage the dip: Analysing research on well-being, happiness, and age, researchers like David Blanchflower and Carol Graham agree that there is a relationship between well-being and age. Their research across multiple countries showed that there is a U-shaped mid-life decline in the level of happiness, well-being, and life satisfaction, which is mostly impacted by disruptive life events such as the loss of a spouse or a job, higher levels of depression, sleep apnoea, and even suicide.[18] The research also suggests that happiness tends to rebound[19]. While some may argue that there is not enough research in this space, the reality is that as a woman in your 40s, you may find yourself juggling some of these life situations. These fluctuations can impact your mood, energy, and overall life satisfaction. If and when you find yourself in the "dip", remember to seek help and support.

Inspire Others: After Naomi Osaka beat Serena Williams in straight sets in the US Open Final in September 2018, different pictures surfaced on the internet. But one picture in particular really caught my attention. It was a picture that she had taken with Serena when she was a lot younger, when she was just a little girl playing tennis. The young talent, Naomi, saw Serena as her idol. She watched her games, aimed to be like her, and worked really hard at it. In her

---

17 Buffet, W. E. (1998). 'Owner's Manual'. Fortune, 137(3), 33
18 https://www.nber.org/system/files/working_papers/w26888/w26888.pdf
19 Is happiness U-shaped everywhere? Age and subjective well-being in 145 countries | Journal of Population Economics (springer.com)

winning speech she acknowledged it was like a dream come true to be playing with her role model, the one person she had always admired. But then, she (Naomi) had been working on herself. She had been diligent until the day came when she walked onto the court with the world's number one. In the end, she won on a global stage! Just like Serena kept showing up, you can inspire others to win when it really matters most. Legacy is a powerful thing.

Welcome to the Big Auntie Squad... you'll love it here.

#8 Application Exercise: Ageism

What is your opinion about ageism?

_____

_____

_____

What are some interesting situations you have experienced since you became Big Auntie?

_____

_____

_____

Who is an inspiring Big Auntie you know, and what can you learn from them?

_____

_____

_____

If you had an "aha" moment completing this exercise, we would love to publish your story! Write to us at www.flourishingforties.com/stories. Your story may be what someone else needs right now.

CHAPTER 8:
Change is Here

"When you're stuck in a spiral, to change all aspects of the spin you only need to change one thing." — Christina Baldwin, author

Our Iceberg is Melting

I love train travel. My best experiences have been on Swiss trains. The Swiss train network is one of the most reliable and sustainable means of transportation in the world. You can bet it will arrive at the platform on time and leave mostly on time. If in doubt, Roger Federer and Trevor Noah's train ride[20] across those stunning landscapes may convince you. I usually carry a book in my handbag when traveling. It comes in handy during long trips.

While on a train ride from Geneva to Bern, looking out the window enjoying the view, I read the book *Our Iceberg is Melting*[21] for the first time. The book tells the remarkable story of a penguin named Fred and an entire colony of penguins as they come to terms

---

20 Grand Train Tour of Switzerland: The ride of a lifetime | Switzerland Tourism (youtube.com)
21 Kotter, J. & Rathgeber, H. (2017). *Our Iceberg is Melting*. Macmillan.

with their "home" melting. Through Fred's leadership and teamwork, the penguins learn how to adapt to change and work together to find a new home.

Cling or Fling?

As I mentioned earlier, in the past 20+ years, my family and I have moved houses a few times. It is never easy. When I hear of or see people who have lived in the same city or same house for years, a part of me wishes I knew exactly what that feels like. When they show me the same bed they've slept on, the school friends they've kept, their neighbourhood cafe, I am grateful on their behalf and sometimes wonder if they fully appreciate what that means. Every time we chose to move to another house or city, it meant a lot of cleaning up, sorting, recycling, scrapping, and giving up a lot of stuff. Sometimes I shed a tear or two, struggling with the decision of what to cling to or fling. However, every time we closed a door to a home and stepped into the front door of another house, it also felt like an adventure and another chance for reinvention.

A few years ago, while testing the idea of "flourishing forties", I partnered with a friend in the United Kingdom to organize a Flourishing Forties business exhibition and networking dinner. That evening, I met Paulina, a senior executive in a global accounting firm. She had a super successful career, having an accelerated rise to the C-Suite before she turned 40, thanks to mentors who spotted her quite early and championed her growth. When I asked if she was apprehensive about change, she responded: "Fofo, I am scared of getting old and being discarded as no longer relevant." She went on to talk about her friend at work who is now over 50, who hasn't had a promotion in years but is too scared to change jobs or career paths for fear of beginning again. Paulina concluded: "I envy the young Gen Zs who have their whole life ahead of them. Lately, I've been thinking I'd hate to become the big Auntie with only stories about her good old days." You can probably guess that we spent the rest of the evening discussing how to "flip the script" when change is inevitable.

I have organized Flourishing Forties networking dinners in other countries too. In Nigeria, I met Romoke, an amazing 47-year-old CEO who lost her high-paying, comfortable 9-5 job when she was barely 41 and now runs several food manufacturing, packaging, and export businesses. When I asked her what keeps her going, she responded: "Fofo, it was hard at first – doubting myself and blaming my boss for firing me. Now, I am so glad I was fired! What keeps me going is the joy of making products that people need and shipping to them anywhere in the world and, most of all, calling the shots myself."

When a life event rocks your world, how do you decide what to hold on to or let go of? What do you do with the mistakes, the successes, the failures, the hurts, the heartache, the break-ups, the accolades, what's working in your life and what's not? How do you choose what to start, stop, or continue? Like a deciduous tree adjusts to changing seasons to survive, you must too. Raising your awareness around changes in your life will help you cope better with them.

The atmosphere when women get together is electrifying. The stories and experiences shared are similar irrespective of the geographical differences – a mix of extraordinary success stories, reinvention, loss, and sometimes stories of anxiety. We plan to co-host a few every year. If you would love to host one in your city, reach out to us.

#9 Application Exercise: Coping with Change

Take a moment to pause and process the following questions.

Where is your iceberg melting away right this minute? Is it related to a child? A job? A marriage? Your dreams? Wealth? Health?

_____
_____
_____

On a scale from 1 to 5, how would you rate the effectiveness of your current support network, and why?

_____
_____
_____

- You are not quite old and you're not as young as you used to be. Admit it.
- You are in a sweet spot that comes with a ton of fun and change.
- You can be surrounded by the messiness of life and still find joy through it.

Whether you've got it all together, are thriving beyond your wildest dreams, or are still trying to find your way, you've still got a whole life ahead of you too. It starts with soaking in the fresh air that a new day brings before you smell your coffee. In this season, you may feel a high level of vibrancy and freedom from within; at other times, your body and emotions may play a few tricks on you. You will experience new things, but that is what makes life an adventure. Don't hold back. Embrace the fullness of your 40s and make the most of it.

Chapter 9:
Embracing Change

*How old would you be if you
didn't know how old you are?"*
—Satchel Paige, professional baseball player

Physical and Hormonal Changes

Being the fourth girl and lastborn of my family, I noticed when my sisters' bodies started to change. I remember asking why my chest was not enlarging like theirs were. I also freaked out a few times when I caught a glimpse of blood during their menstrual periods and worried a lot whenever any of my sisters had very painful cramps. I didn't understand why they had so much pain, but I remember my mum's home therapy techniques that helped them cope during those five or so days each month.

My mum has always been a great teacher. As we grew up under her care, as far back as I can remember, she would spend time with me and my three sisters telling us stories and giving us advice about life as a woman. I remember her schooling us about feminine hygiene and economical alternatives to sanitary pads, as we couldn't afford the best products all the time. So, when I sighted my first period while on vacation at a cousin's place far away from home, I was not alarmed. As young as I was, I knew exactly what to do. I was too embarrassed to ask my male cousin for help. His family probably didn't notice they were running out of toilet tissue, which became my saving grace for the two months I spent at their house. I was so proud of myself, but the menstrual pain was real.

In my work coaching women over 40, sometimes, we uncover that changes in body shape and size can impact self-esteem and confidence, which triggers a focus on fitness and self-care. Feeling gorgeous? Fatigued? Fabulous? No different? During this season, expect your body to go through some little changes. This could range from physical changes such as weight gain or loss, hormonal changes leading to mood swings, lower or higher sex drive and dry vagina, sleep abnormalities, and potentially overall feelings of vitality. It's harder to find the courage to dare new dreams, try new goals, and make yourself proud.

One of the significant shifts you may start to experience are perimenopausal symptoms. The menopausal transition is usually characterised by irregular periods which typically begins in the mid40s and culminates in menopause, which signifies the end of the natural reproductive phase for a woman.

When menopause is eventually reached, some of the common symptoms reported are hot flushes, night sweats, and genitourinary discomfort, low sex drive, weight gain (abdominal fat), fatigue, mood swings, and changes in metabolic health. If you are experiencing any significant changes in your body, consult your GP. Many symptoms of menopause can be helped with the right medical advice. We no longer have to suffer in silence.

Mental and Emotional Changes

Psychologists define mental health as the combination of emotional, psychological, and social well-being. It encompasses the way you think, your feelings, decision making, the way you build relationships, and how you cope with positive and negative emotions. During this season, you will go through different transition phases that will challenge all these areas of yourself. How you cope through the changes determines your well-being.[22]

Some people are naturally more resilient than others. The reverse can also be the case. My hope is that as you read this, you find enough love and support around you enough to dig through the tunnel of life and find the light that has always waited for you on the other side.

Social and Relational Changes

Certain relationships and social circles from your yesterday may begin to melt away. Maybe that has happened already. Like a deciduous tree that sheds its leaves in the autumn, there are some relationships you may have to actively detach from. Leaves falling off gives room for new leaves springing up and blossoming in spring and summer. Not everyone connected to you right now is a part of your new process. Stop holding on to people or things that have no place in the future you desire.

Take the time to assess your social circles. Some may become toxic to your health and your fruits, and eventually will affect your roots. In the neuroscience of change, studies[23] have shown that

---

23 https://doi.org/10.1016/j.neubiorev.2020.12.002

positive feelings and emotions are building blocks for cultivating joy, resilience, and a state of flourishing, which influence physical and emotional well-being. Develop relationships that will nurture your roots and nourish your growth. Beware of friends in social circles who want you to remain at the level you have outgrown.

Embracing Change – Time to Push

When a pregnant woman goes into labour, most times it is because the time is right for that baby to experience a whole new world of growth When the labour pangs become stronger, you don't stop. You push!! It's like the baby telling you "Ready or not, Mum, here I come", and wherever you are, whoever is with you at that very moment, the focus is on *nothing but the push!* A change is about to happen that will impact not only your life, but the baby's and anyone else's connected to that change.

Similarly, when it is fruiting season for a tree, the fruits appear. The tree cannot say "Hey, I'm not ready yet." When the time is ripe, fruits – be it mango, apples, or peaches, mature and are in position, ready to be plucked or processed, bringing healthy nutrition, joy, and happy moments to those who partake of it. If the tree could see the smiles on the faces of little children eating juicy mangoes or you enjoying your favourite smoothie, it would be so proud of itself.

#10 Application Exercise: Pushing Season

As you chug along in your 40s:

What is the best thing you could ever imagine happening to you in this decade?

_____

_____

_____

How can you leverage this season of change to strengthen your relationships and build deeper connections?

_____

_____

_____

If you experience a severe physical, hormonal, social, or emotional change, what will be your go-to strategy?

_____

_____

_____

Who or What can you lean on in your "pushing" season?

_____

_____

_____

Chapter 10:
Failing Forward

"You're over the top when you know that success does not make you and failure does not break you" —Zig Ziglar, salesman and motivational speaker

"What would you do if you knew you couldn't fail?" This is a common question motivational gurus ask when trying to get us to think and act differently. I think this question can be misinterpreted to imply that failure obstructs success.

Growing up, I believed that failing was a negative thing. I remember holding my mid-high school report in my hands. I had As in 7 subjects and a C in my mother-tongue language subject, and I wouldn't go home because all I saw on that paper was a failure to pass my own mother tongue and a scolding or maybe even a beating for not having straight As.

In my second year, I looked at the results ranking in Pharmacy school; for the first time in my academic life, I was not in the top four. I cried the whole day, wondering what had gone wrong. The school system taught me that failure was the opposite of success and that failing meant you disappointed many people.

Several years of experience and rewiring of my brain have taught me that failure is success if you learn something from it. Like the time I forgot to thoroughly scrutinize a production report before releasing tons of products for export, only to have to deal with a multi-country product recall a year later because we missed some important stability data, which we could have caught if someone on the team had paid more attention and I had reviewed carefully before signing off. That error cost the company thousands of dollars and my team many sleepless nights. I showed up on daily calls explaining to stakeholders what we were doing to manage company reputation and customer credibility. That season in my career seemed impossible to come back from, but I cannot forget something one of my senior directors said to me one day when I wanted to quit. He said, "What has this painful process taught you?" Then he said, "Are you just going to throw that away too?" In over two decades of working in corporate, the most accelerated growth I have experienced has been working in companies where it is safe to fail and experiment.

Failing forward for you could mean:

- Learning to forgive yourself for the times you didn't know better.
- Realizing that it's okay to change your mind and even career paths - it's called growth.
- Shifting from trying to be perfect to realising your imperfections only make you uniquely you.
- Realizing that the revolution in your spirit will only lead to an evolution of your soul's true purpose.

Enough of the mantra that "40 is the new 20". I dare say "40 is the new 40". We are changing the narratives and redefining what women over 40 look like, feel like, dream of, and contribute to the world. It doesn't mean we stop dreaming - we simply stopped daydreaming and intentionally work towards the dreams we desire. Some days, I feel like wonder woman, and other days, I'm just grateful I made it through - both are wins in themselves.

"Failure-Prone" Thinking	"Failing Forward" Thinking
I'm not good enough.	I am good enough and can get better.
It can't be done.	Maybe it can't be done yet. I'll start and get help.
I'm not an expert.	I know enough to start.
I'm too shy.	Confidence rises as I move.
Who am I to aim high?	Who will I become if I don't aim high?
I'm too young/too old.	Skilled people never lack. They create opportunities.
What if I fail?	Failure is a steppingstone.
When the going gets tough, the tough quit.	When the going gets tough, the tough collaborate and re-strategize.

How often do you celebrate your little milestones/wins during a change? Rarely, frequently, or consistently?

Top Gun: Maverick is an adrenalin-pumping film where Captain Pete "Maverick", played by Tom Cruise, is ordered to get a new generation of fighter pilots ready for a very dangerous mission. One of the trainee pilots is the son of his late friend "Goose", who died while with him on a mission about 30 years earlier. On his first official meeting with the elite graduates of Top Gun school, Maverick, as he was fondly called, challenged the thinking of these ambitious fighters to ditch everything they had learned from the flight school manual. He stresses his point by throwing the big operational manual into the wastebin. In his words, "Your enemy knows that manual too. What the enemy does not know is your limits." What a profound statement!

Let me ask you – What's your limit?

I don't believe anyone can truly tell you that.

How far can or will you go in this season of your life?

Deep down, only you can answer that question.

You already know about some of the most successful creatives who have inspired our world with their fighting spirits and failing forward approach. Should I remind you about Walt Disney, who, despite failed businesses and bankruptcy, believed in his creative vision which continues to inspire the world of entertainment and motion pictures? Do you need to be reminded about Vera Wang, who entered the fashion world at the age of 40, or Wangari Maathai, who founded the Green Belt Movement in her 40s, championing environmental and women's rights? All pushed forward, against all odds.

Fear is human nature and a vital part of our survival instinct. If I knew I couldn't fail, I could come up with a list of things I would do.

But does that mean I would take that list and start ticking off the wishes right way? Do I feel equipped to do so? Is time on my side or working against me?

The American Psychology Association defines fear of failure as an unshakeable anxiety about failing to attain self-inflicted or external standards and goals. Fear of failure is ranked among the top three reasons people do not reach their fullest potential or fulfil their purpose on earth.

A few things to remember:

1. **You are not a failure:** There is a difference in failing at something and *being* a failure. It can be hard to accept failure and move on from it, especially the failure you were not expecting – for example, a failed business, a failed marriage, a failed idea – the ones that cost you something significant you might never get back. But here is a reminder: you *failed* – you are not *a failure*. Carefully review the reasons behind the failure without self-reduction.

2. **You are not your failure:** The fact that you failed does not mean you rename yourself the failure. When "Iceman" challenged "Maverick" in the movie *Top Gun-Maverick* as he struggled with the "It's time to let go" Iceman typed on his computer, Maverick responded, "I don't know how." Eventually, what saved his life and helped them achieve the mission was an inner drive to succeed and move past his resistance to forgive himself, trust his competence and his immature wingman, and mentor his team. Do not allow

your failures to hold you back from the limitless possibilities and successes that await you.

3. **Failure is inevitable:** Living life like you are walking on eggshells is not the best way to live your life; neither is expecting to fail at whatever you try. What makes you come alive? Find the courage to attempt it. The faster you fail, the closer you are to a successful breakthrough. Surround yourself with a supportive network and mentors who have experienced failure and overcome it. Before hopping onto the next shiny thing, try polishing what's in your hand.

4. **Failure is not the end:** A baby learning to walk will fall repeatedly, cry sometimes, land on their bum sometimes, but get up and keep trying. A baby who refuses to get up after falling may miss timing and the thrills from those watching and cheering her on.

The choices you make today – your willingness to grow, and your ability to fail and bounce back to try again – will give you a better chance of enjoying the life you are living today and what is ahead.

"If you think you can or you think you can't, then you are probably right."
—Henry Ford, industrialist and engineer

When next you experience a failure or a "turbulence", don't forget to put on your oxygen mask first before helping others, and strap on your life jacket so it is easier to float above the setbacks. When the comfortable becomes uncomfortable, open your arms to change. Do not hesitate to slide down the ramp and launch into the future that awaits you on the other side of fear.

The beautiful thing about being a *fortician* is that you have had some failures along the way. How you deal or dealt with these setbacks will influence how purposeful and successful your life will be in the present and the future. Why not create a "'failure album" to capture some of your biggest failures and what you learned from them?

It is easier to read the stories of celebrities online, but you, dear reader, are a celebrity too. I would love to hear your own stories of triumph and failing forward. Be a guest on our podcast show or drop a message with your story https://www.flourishingforties.com/stories. We would love to review and share your story to inspire many more that the 40s and beyond are a brilliant time to be alive!

In your 40s, your fight is different... **push!**

There's so much more to live for. Beyond the success, the accolades, or the pain...push! Do something that's hard to do and see how strong you really are. You are the perfect woman for such a time as this and, deep down inside, you know it.

#11 Application Exercise: The Wake-Up Call

Do you always feel you have to be in control of everything?
_____
_____
_____

What is a dream you've been holding on to for years?
_____
_____

Are you actively pushing it through or waiting for the perfect time?
_____
_____
_____

In what area of life can you fail forward this year?
_____
_____
_____

CHAPTER 11:
Managing the Blues

You owe yourself the love that you so freely give to other people."
– Alexandra Elle, wellness educator

For forticians, experiencing the blues can be triggered at any time. The "blues" can be described as those moments when you are stuck in a funk – feeling down, sad, stressed, or just kind of blah! I have been there and maybe you have too. Everyone from time to time experiences the "blues" and it is usually temporary (within the context of emotions that are not as intense as clinical depression). I once had a girlfriend who was a brilliant food journalist and TV host tell me, "Ageing in this industry feels like an uphill battle. It is sometimes hard to keep up with all the travel, now that I've got two big potatoes (kids) in my bag. A male colleague with grey hair is judged as experienced and wise; a woman with grey hair is judged as an older lady. It takes a lot to keep up appearances."

Other triggers women over 40 have told me about include:

- Your business suddenly collapsing due to bad decisions or circumstances completely out of your control

- Being passed over for promotion at work and replaced by a younger colleague or new hire.

- Looking in the mirror and seeing new wrinkles creeping in, a change in skin elasticity, or grey hair in visible areas.

- Dealing with the reality of a divorce when all you dreamed about as a Disney fanatic was getting married to your knight in shining armour and growing old together.

- Battling an illness due to ageing and feeling left out of the fun you used to enjoy.

- Losing a job, meaning you have to adjust your lifestyle and downsize your standard of living.

- Working in a high-stress corporate environment where you cannot bring your "whole self" to work to avoid being labelled different.

- Trying to study at night to earn your degree because daytime has you juggling a career and ageing parents.

- Feeling you don't deserve your success because you are surrounded by people from your past who are living an average life.

- Realising the responsibilities of being a wife or a mum mean you cannot just flyaway and go on a girls' weekend like before.

- Working very hard to climb the career ladder, but then noticing that now you're at the top of your game, it doesn't feel enough. You feel lonely and isolated, even though you have lots of mentees and thousands of followers.

When you find yourself experiencing the blues

Check your expectations: Is there an expectation you are trying to live up to that seems to be triggering the blues? Sometimes when I catch myself feeling agitated or anxious, I ask myself if I am downplaying the woman I have become or if I am judging myself by someone else's standards.

Check your environment: The blues can be triggered by fatigue, overwhelm, or stress. Shifting your thoughts from that environment in that moment could bring you some relief. At some point, I changed my environment, my workplace, and joined new social networks and fitness club to continue to inspire myself and rise beyond feeling like the "smartest or optimistic person" in my circle.

Check your communication: In this season of your life, the general assumption is that you already have a fair idea about your strengths, your superpowers, your unique style, and how to deal with difficult situations. If that's a tick, tick, and tick for you, *you go, girl*! I celebrate you. If that's not you, be vulnerable to share what works for you with family and friends. Often, when life changes, it's natural to assume that everyone else should have noticed. Generally, this is not the case. It is critical to communicate your choices to the relevant people in your life – family members, business associates, significant partners, customers, or clients. People cannot read your mind. You have to let them know what help looks like.

Construct stepping goals: If you are struggling with the goals you've set for yourself, review them. Could you break the tasks down into smaller steps that are easier to achieve? Do you need to delegate some steps to someone else, so you move faster? Do you need a business or career coach to help you overcome limiting beliefs? By asking the right questions and seeking guidance from wise mentors, you can tap into your inner juices and evaluate your options.

Embrace Your flawbulousity: Embrace the woman you are. Flaws + Fabulous = Flawbulousity! Some of us don't know how to enjoy what we have in the present. We are bogged down by what happened yesterday and hustling every day for the future we desire, and we sometimes forget to breathe in and let go. There's someone out there who craves something you do so effortlessly you don't even think it's a superpower.

Embrace counselling: If you struggle with more severe symptoms of depression, seek professional support. Find a trusted counsellor, psychologist, or GP and discuss how you feel. Book an appointment right away. Don't waste any more time not enjoying this amazing decade of your life.

You can also help a friend who you suspect may be experiencing the blues by asking any of the above questions. Create a safe space for a conversation and check in with them in an empathetic way. It may trigger an awareness that leads to healing and recovery. If they express thoughts of self-harm or worse, encourage them to contact a mental health hotline or seek professional support immediately. You may be saving a life.

Here are some other helpful tips for managing the temporary blues. Want a downloadable PDF? It is available in the Flourishing Forties Community Vault.

Triggers	Strategies for Managing the Blues
Physical	• Establish a structured routine with a sense of purpose. • Incorporate regular breaks and exercise into your routine. • Mindful eating and balanced diet for overall well-being.
Spiritual	• Take prayer walks, sing out loud, read the Bible or other uplifting books that feed your spirit and stir up hope.
Mental	• Practise deep breathing and mindful journalling • Incorporate a bed-time routine and a healthy sleep pattern. • Engage in activities that stimulate your cognitive ability, like reading, puzzles, crafts, coding, and creating something. • Don't take life too seriously – learn to "live light" and incorporate some humour in your life!
Financial	• Find a financial advisor, tax expert, or accountant to help you plan your present and your future properly. • Leverage appropriate schemes that give you financial stability and multiply generational wealth for your loved ones.
Social	• Find support groups, and engage in community events around you. • Travel to new places from time to time to meet new people.

	- Use technology to stay connected with family and friends. - Detox your relationships and cut out what no longer serves you
Hobbies and interests	- Explore new activities and hobbies for enjoyment. - Join groups or classes to meet like-minded people and individuals with a totally different view from yours.
Professional support	- Empower yourself with helpful information to help deal with it. - Consult with a psychologist or counsellor to help deal with the blues. - Join professional networks to keep stimulating your passion.
Lack of purpose	- Engage in activities that align with your values. - Seek a coach, counsellor, or mentor. - Volunteer and help others in need – it gives you perspective. - Create a purpose bucket-list and vision board.
Grief and loss	- Allow yourself to grieve and seek support when needed. - Share feelings with friends, family, or a professional counsellor. - Loss is not the end – you can hope again.
Relationships	- Develop a strong social support network that nourishes you.

	• Join or create support groups for women facing similar life transitions.
Flourishing lifestyle	• Laugh often – it is proven to be good medicine for the soul. • Focus on the positive aspects of ageing. • Cultivate gratitude by acknowledging daily blessings.

In my thirties, I remember having dinner with a group of older girlfriends in their 40s, and we were talking about the changes our skin would go through as we grew older. One of them said, "Wait till you hit 45; that's when everything starts going downhill," as if to scare the rest of us from aging any further. Fast forward to now: I'm 40 plus, and spoiler alert, I haven't fallen off a cliff yet. But let's be real - there is a lot that people do not talk about in this phase of life. For example – your skin. There's a billion-dollar industry out there waiting to sell us the latest magical cream. Don't get me wrong. I'm all for a good serum. But here's the truth – skin changes. That glow of your 20s? It may take a little more effort than before to maintain it. You thought weightlifting was only for athletes? Now we all know that maintaining muscle tone is a smart thing to do in your 40s.

Some of us have thriving careers. Some of us can't seem to figure out what's next. The sheer pressure to reinvent yourself on Monday, find your passion on Tuesday, and build a brand out of it by Thursday, is all around us. If you fall in this category, here's what no one tells you but I will because we are now besties - It is okay if your career isn't shiny and perfect at 45. Some of us are still figuring it out.

The world is noisy with shiny success stories, but sometimes, real life is a little more complex. Get up, get dressed, and get help. You get to decide how you want your next chapter to go.

Living life as a woman over 40 isn't perfect, but it also is not the cliff we have been led to believe, either. There is so much freedom, so much love, so much clarity, and so much more to live for. Feeling lonely? It is an opportunity to make new friends (quality over quantity). Lost a job? There is still time to find a new one, partner with someone else, or start something for yourself. Don't waste any more precious time staring at a list of "should-haves" and "could-be." It's time to G.R.O.W.

- **Ground yourself** in who you really are, where you've been, and where you are going.
- **Release** what no longer serves you or fits with where you are going.
- **Open your mind and heart** to new possibilities and dreams you may have benched.
- **Wake up** every morning and get to **work** towards your new vision.

Whether you are in a stage of seeding, rooting, growing, blooming, or renewing, you can flourish in your season. Your best is yet to come.

#12: APPLICATION EXERCISE: Check-In

On a scale from 1 to 10, how have you been feeling lately?

_____

_____

Any changes in your sleep patterns or energy levels that concern you?

_____

_____

Have you experienced a loss or major life change recently?

_____

_____

How are you coping with your recent failure or disappointment?

_____

_____

How often do you long for past interests and activities that used to bring you pleasure?

_____

_____

Do you feel a sense of hopelessness or that things won't get better?

_____

_____

Is there a specific aspect of your life causing you prolonged stress or worry?

_____

_____

PART THREE
Autumn: Thriving Still

A Woman Reborn

Losing control, tangled in shadows

Lost in a world that feels upside down

The emptiness of the hour

The waning of power

How in the world did I get here?

Would someone catch me?

Will someone hold me?

Is anyone listening as my dreams fade away?

What do I seek? What will I find?

How will it be? What must I do?

The questions race through my mind

Like a swift wind of hurricane

I am leaving the familiar behind

A life I cannot rewind

Forward I will crawl

In time, I will run

Wait a minute…is that rain?

Yes, at last, it is a downpour

Each droplet a promising gain

Exposing things, too hard to ignore

I'll embrace the fall

And heed destiny's call

In the chaos of rain, I'll find my way

A woman reborn, like the breaking of day.

© *Mofoluwaso Ilevbare*

Chapter 12:
Equipped for Every Season

"There is freedom waiting for you, on the breezes of the sky, and you ask—what if I fall? Oh but my darling, what if you fly?"
—Erin Hanson, poet

Some parts of the world experience four different seasons in a calendar year – spring, summer, autumn, and winter. Metaphorically, springtime connotes newness, growth, a fresh start, rejuvenation, and burst of energy in your life. There may be a few firsts like a career pivot, a new job, new-found love life, starting a business, becoming single again, being your own CEO, having a baby, prioritising your health for once, or more. In your 40s, you may start getting to know yourself on a whole new level. If you're in the spring season of your 40s, enjoy the ride and make the most of every moment. It can be both overwhelming and exciting at the same time. For example, the reproductive changes you may begin to experience are exciting new beginnings and certainly not the end.

Then comes summertime – a time to relish sunshine, joy, freedom, and love. Summertime is usually a time to travel and explore the world, deepen relationships, and celebrate vigour and vitality. It is also a season where emotions can flare up due to the intensity of expression. Communication and conflict management skills can help you weather the heat of arguments and disagreements. If you are in the summer season of your 40s, enjoy the colourful beauty life brings.

A third season you may experience in your 40s can be likened to autumn. This season is also referred to as fall. The fall season of life can feel like a time of drift, dryness, and disruption.

Discolouration

Deciduous trees get environmental cues in the autumn. Science tells us that senescence (a natural and gradual ageing process) starts to take place. As daylight decreases and temperatures drop, this process triggers the breakdown of chlorophyll molecules (the green pigment responsible for photosynthesis), revealing other pigments in the leaves, such as carotenoids and anthocyanins, in the form of orange, brownish, or reddish colours previously masked by chlorophyll. Reducing chlorophyll allows trees to preserve energy, store nutrients, and prepare for winter.

Detachment

Growing up, we loved watching a reality TV show called "Hoarders", where clutter professionals swoop into the home of someone who cannot let go of stuff and try to untangle them from piles of clutter, freeing them to live life differently. Watching the struggles at the start of the show and the physical, mental, and emotional detachment by the end is always fascinating. The hoarders often end up in tears as they learn to embrace freedom and a breath of fresh air in their environment. Deciduous trees don't hesitate to remove what's no longer needed when the seasons change.

Distribution

As deciduous trees start to conserve energy, they redistribute nutrients in preparation for winter. While energy production levels are high in summer, a tree knows that a time of scarcity is coming, and to survive, it must be smart. It prepares for dormancy and gets ready for the transition process. Things may seem dull and sad during autumn, but remember, it is only for a season.

Degradation

Autumn signals the ageing and death of certain plant tissues, especially in leaves. By undergoing cellular changes, the tree can re-absorb valuable nutrients from ageing tissues and redistribute them to other parts of the plant, such as new leaves or developing seeds. This process of degradation helps plants prepare for periods of stress (in this case, winter) and helps the tree adapt to changing environmental conditions. The blend of colours creates scenery that you won't see any other time of the year.

Lessons from Autumn

- **There's beauty in you:** Experiencing "autumn" may not feel like the best time of your life; yet if you look deep enough, you may experience the unmasking of new gifts and virtues you didn't even know you had within you. Amuse yourself. Appreciate the richness of your many colours and embrace them. Protect your energy levels. Rediscover *you* in every season.

- **Let it go:** Autumn may represent a season of shedding old habits, decluttering your physical, mental, social, or emotional spaces. You may need to rearrange your priorities so you can get unstuck. Freedom is calling out your name. Will you answer the call? You can't stretch your hands to accept a new gift if your hands are full.

- **Prepare:** Always be prepared for a rainy day. Diversify your resources – time, energy, money, projects, investments, connections, or knowledge. Keep developing a portfolio of skills and networks, and add what you can into your "toolbox" of life. You never know when you may need a hammer or a safety pin.

- **Silence is golden:** Sometimes, when going through a transition, hibernation is necessary. When you plant a seed in the soil, it seems for many days nothing is happening. Don't mistake hibernation for inactivity. Not everything in your life needs to be aired in public spaces. Carve out time to prepare for a new chapter in your life and choose rest over chaos.

- **·Growth demands change:** Change can be hard to adjust to. A tree in autumn is impacted by winds and has to sway from side to side to maintain its stability. As the weather changes and routines are disrupted, you may find yourself pulled in different directions, tested on all sides, seemingly spinning out of control.

Some questions to ponder on:

"What aspects of this change can I control?"

"Who could be an anchor to support me?"

"What worked for me the last time I experienced a change?"

"What opportunities might arise if I embrace this change?

It will be spring again

When you are going through stressful situations, often it seems impossible to imagine that one day it will all be over and you will laugh again. Whatever "falling leaves" signifies to you in this season, trust the process, knowing that, in a little while, seasons will change and new buds will sprout again. Celebrating the golden 50s, post-menopause, empty nesting, financial and other freedoms can be good things to look forward to.

I remember the first time my son's tooth fell out. He was puzzled and cried a lot. I kept calming him down, telling him that a tooth would come in to replace it, but all his tongue could feel was the ugly gap. A few weeks passed and his tongue brushed against his gum and he felt something growing in the gap. He ran to my room screaming "It's growing, Mum!" I chuckled and said "I told you." The year he turned 10, he lost seven of his teeth in quick succession – only this time, whenever one fell out, he would grab the tooth and hand it over to show me before gargling with some water and then running off to play.

The *Collins English Dictionary* defines "bloom" as "a healthy, vigorous, or flourishing condition", a term used to describe when a plant comes into its full beauty or health. What do you need to bloom? Download the B.L.O.O.M. resource from the Flourishing Forties Community vault.

I listened as Dianne relayed her story. Being a perfectionist, she had been forced to confront her reality that sometimes, life doesn't go according to plan. Her magical rise to power and prestige before the age of 40 was beginning to crumble. She was starting to feel stagnant, with no drive to pursue her career ambitions. On top of that, she was experiencing what she thought could be perimenopausal symptoms, but every time she visited her doctor, all she was ever told was to get some rest. She then decided to go on a 3-month sabbatical from work. This was a big deal for someone like her who hardly took a break. She found a new sense of purpose and joy. She embraced the fact that her worth was not tied to her LinkedIn accolades or the size of her waistline. In the *autumn* season of life, you don't have to prove anything to anyone. It's a game-changer. Redefine your version of success. You can be a masterpiece and a work in progress at the same time.

Whatever season you are in, you can BLOOM.

CHAPTER 13:
Transform Your Habits, Transform Your Life

*"Motivation is what gets you started.
Habits are what keeps you going."*
—*Jim Rohn, motivational speaker*

Knowing who you are in a world that constantly wants to categorise you and dictate who you should be, what you should do, or how you should feel, is critical to blooming in every season of your life.

When the purpose of a thing is not clear, it can be misused. Picture trying to use a blade to cut a tree. A blade cuts through something but its purpose is different from that of a chainsaw. By creating an inspiring vision and executing your plan with discipline, you can trigger behaviours and actions that reinforce your identity.

What you focus on, grows. What you spend time on, magnifies. When you live in the present, you are living where life is happening and have the power to determine to an extent how the future could turn out.

How to cultivate better habits

Some habits are easier to form than others. After nearly 15,000 days on earth, I dare say you've formed some pretty good habits and probably some bad ones too. For the next season of your life, I challenge you to level up on your habits, especially the good ones you have been struggling with. You know you should exercise but you find yourself constantly drawn to three hours of Netflix and feel guilty afterwards. You know you should work on your brand and grow your business, but you find yourself spiralling in comparison, stacking up what every other person is doing. The day is done, you roll into bed, and you say, "I'll do it tomorrow."

The good news is that you can form new habits. The neuroplastic nature of the brain makes it possible for your brain to be reprogrammed allowing you to change behaviour.

American journalist Charles Duhigg[24] described the three components of the habit loop: cue, routine, and reward. Another American writer, James Clear, expanded this concept in his book *Atomic Habits* into a four-stage process: cue-craving-response-reward. A cue is the trigger or signal that initiates the domino effect.

Five Examples of Cues:

1. **Environmental**: Healthy snacks on the office desk might cue the habit of healthy snacking during work hours versus walking to the nearby donut shop.
2. **Emotional**: Emotions such as joy, anger and worry, can trigger habitual behaviour.

---

24 https://www.charlesduhigg.com/the-power-of-habit

3. **Internal**: Our physiological responses to cues can lead to the reinforcement of certain habits.

4. **Time bound**: Performing specific tasks repeatedly at specific certain times of the day, week, or month can be cues for habit formation.

5. **Behaviour**: Finishing up at work might cue the habit of changing into workout gear and heading to the gym.

When we engage in a habitual routine triggered by a cue, motivated by a craving, and complemented by a reward, our brain develops neurological pathways which, over time, become more efficient, making the behaviour increasingly automatic. During the reward phase, our brain releases dopamine (also known as the feel-good neurotransmitter), which further binds the cue with the routine.

In his book *Atomic Habits*, James Clear[25] described how making small incremental changes he termed "atomic habits" can have a lasting impact on behaviour. Using the concept of habit stacking, the author delved into the role of the basal ganglia (a set of structures located in the brain) in habit formation and explained how our identity (your conviction of who you are) and environment can shape our behaviour through repeated actions which then become automated patterns we display.

---

25 Atomic Habits: Tiny Changes, Remarkable Results by James Clear

Create a Habit Inventory

Understanding the habits you have formed over time can help you understand why you behave the way you do. For example, you may notice that you are always on time for meetings, you find it easy to forgive others, you eat junk food whenever you are stressed, or that when you wake up every morning, your first action is reaching for your phone so you can scroll through the *Financial Times* or cable networks to catch up on global business updates.

Do a Why-Why Analysis

Once you have made an inventory of your most repetitive habits, do a why-why analysis. A why-why analysis is a simple process for getting to the root cause of an issue by asking yourself the question why about four or five times. When reviewing your habit inventory list, ask yourself "Why do I behave this way?" Whatever your first answer is, ask yourself why again. It is a powerful word – children know this better than most. "Why?" is as powerful as it is annoying. It could destabilise your entire reasoning process and make you question your beliefs. That is the hard work I want you to do here. You may not even be able to answer why you do some things you do. This is because they've been wired into your brain over time and show up as a behaviour. How did I come about this behaviour? Who taught me and when? Some of your habits will date back to your childhood and what you learned in school, church, or local community.

Conduct a Habit Effectiveness Audit

You can also assess your habits using a habit effectiveness checklist to check improvements you have made and make further adjustments.

Ask yourself:

- "How is this behaviour serving me?"
- "What is the impact of my behaviour on others?"

When you understand the habit loop, it will be easier to modify the behaviour. Here's a simple example. I used to have a habit of often frantically looking for the car keys whenever I wanted to go out, or I might be out and about and then realise I have forgotten my wallet or mobile phone. By simply putting physical cues in place – key holders on the wall – gradually, I knew where to find my keys and where to place them. One other little cue I learned from my sister was to say the words "phone, wallet, keys" before I stepped out the door. It was funny the first time I heard her say those words when we stayed at their house for summer vacation. When she repeated this a few times, I asked her why. It was for the same reasons I mentioned already. Today, I don't even have to say the words anymore. They are engraved in my subconscious, and I hardly ever leave the house without my phone, wallet, and keys.

It is possible and really quite easy to reprogram your subconscious in lots of beneficial ways.

Replace Old Habits

Once you have assessed your habits, you may notice one or two habits that are detrimental to who you have decided to become. If there is no motivation or long-term benefit, you may ignore the red flags. Challenge yourself. Take time to understand the elements that created each habit loop in the first place. What was the cue that led to a craving, which elicited a reward, and then became a routine? The same way new habits are not easily formed, bad ones are not easily broken either. You have to work at it with determination.

- Begin with clearly articulating and visualising the better outcome you are looking for and the new identity you want to take on.

- Then, gradually create different and attractive cues that can motivate change. Start small, if you have to.

- Break down the process into small manageable milestones.

- Anchor your new cues on an already existing habit for support.

- Find accountability partners or role models that can spur you to change. Create mini rewards for each milestone to further encourage you to change.

The best way to break bad habits is to replace them with better ones.

Track Your New Habits

Habit trackers are useful tools to help you visualize progress and develop accountability. These trackers can be paper-based or e-applications powered by technology. When my son was younger, he would regularly lose his lunch box, school sweater, or water bottle. His items were a constant find at the "lost and found" section in school. Using a habit tracker helped him develop the habit of taking responsibility and care for his personal items, and once in a while when he loses something, he immediately feels bad about it and adjusts his behaviour the next day.

A strategy that works for me is not viewing my habits as achievement goals, but rather as progressive behavioural change. For example, I noticed that when I set goals like "I want to lose 5 kg in 30 days", I sometimes have achieved that goal but dropped off the scale in a few weeks or months. There was a drive to achieve it, but the process I followed did not help me build sustainable habits. It is within the unfolding of life's journey that we discover our greatest truths and find true meaning.

Connect With the Little You

Before I started worrying about puberty, boys, and periods, I remember being that cheerful little girl who wore pink-checkered pinafores and played football barefooted. As a grown woman and a mum, I have learned to let go of childish behaviour. Good old photo albums of my childhood or Google photos that pop up on my mobile remind me from time to time of the little girl inside me called Mofoluwaso. Being the only C-suite woman in a leadership team several times, the only female manager in a group several times, sometimes the only black woman speaker at an event, or one of the minority on many occasions has been a constant part of my career journey.

My experiences growing up as a little girl and the confidence and resilience instilled in me by my parents have driven a lot of my gender empowerment work today in high schools and professional settings. I believe that even though it is still predominantly a man's world, it's a woman's world too. Who were you at five, or six, or seven? What did you enjoy doing? Many years ago, when I asked myself that question, I recalled my passion for reading, writing, and assisting others. At each stage of my development, I was told I displayed leadership qualities.

In primary and secondary schools, I was usually class captain or head girl/head prefect and represented my school in many science or mathematics competitions. I was a choir director in university, a Sunday school team leader, a girl's scout, and even a cultural dance troupe leader at one point. I recalled that family members told me that, as a little girl, I would scout people's houses for newspapers, books, or magazine articles I could find, then curl up in the pile and lose myself in a world of reading while every other kid was playing.

Inside each one of us is that little girl that loved to ask questions and explore the world around her. That brave little girl may be the daughter of a princess and had everything she could ever want in life. That brave little girl may also have been born in difficult times with no silver spoon in her mouth. Wherever you fall on the spectrum of brave little girls, one thing unites us all. You are *still* here, and that is priceless!

As you mature and grow into the strong, brave mid-life version of the woman that you are, be careful not to let go of the playful, fun-loving, little girl inside. Learn to connect with her from time to time. Let her remind you to laugh when life gets tough. Let her remind you to ask for help when you get stuck. Above all, let her remind you that you matter!

Define Success on Your Own Terms

Everyone has a back story, but what sells magazines is the front cover or cover story. Have you ever read stories of successful people who apparently enjoyed overnight success? One trend you will find in their stories is that they start with self-belief and an action that led to success. Finding your inner warrior is key to maximising your decade and achieving big dreams. Motivation will take you a few steps daily. Your *why* will keep you going for years and may outlive you. To grow, you must learn to accept the curve balls that life throws at you, roll a big fist, and throw them right back. You must learn to embrace change, push past your comfort zone, and go in search of a new treasure island.

As an advocate for more-women-in-leadership, I've seen many women drop off the leadership grid or resign from boards post maternity leave or due to family responsibilities like taking care of aging parents, managing family loss, fatigue, and prolonged burnout. There are also many women who have been caught between bad leadership and the politics of the *"glass cliff syndrome"* [26] and lost opportunities. When it comes to what truly makes us happy and brings career and life fulfillment, there is no one-size-fits-all answer.

Human science has proven that when we are about to step into an unfamiliar territory, we often feel some jitters. It is natural. However, many of us mistake this natural feeling—so rather than embrace it and use it to fuel our learning and growth process, we jump ship and prolong our breakthrough. Other times, society undermines our feminine leadership skills, calling them "soft"

---

[26] https://www.bbc.com/future/article/20220204-the-danger-of-the-glass-cliff-for-women-and-people-of-colour

through the lens of bias. But you can choose today to be different. Not just for yourself, but for others, born and unborn, whose destinies and breakthroughs are tied to yours.

What does success feel like to you?

_____

_____

_____

When you say you want success, what does it look like to you?

_____

_____

_____

Picture it and write it down.

Success has no one universal definition. It means different things to different people. This is why you cannot measure success through my lens or other people's view of the world. You may never measure up.

#13 Application Exercise: Reframing Perceived Weaknesses

What do you do when you feel you have more weaknesses than strengths? You can ignore them altogether and not waste any time on them. I used to cringe or go into self-denial anytime someone dared mention that I might have a weakness.

During job interviews, candidates dread that question: "Tell me about your weakness/What would you say you are not good at?"

The truth is we all have at least one area of opportunity, or weakness. When I started to reframe my thinking around my weaknesses, I stopped viewing them as a show-stopper. Let me show you how.

Think about three attributes you consider a weakness (or something people constantly tell you is a weakness).

#1: _____

In what situation has this/can this so-called weakness come in handy?

_____

_____

What support system (people, tech, process) can help you bloom despite this weakness?

_____

_____

#2: _____

In what situation has this/can this so-called weakness come in handy?

_____

_____

What support system (people, tech, process) can help you bloom despite this weakness?

_____

_____

#3: _____

In what situation has this/can this so-called weakness come in handy?

_____

_____

What support system (people, tech, process) can help you bloom despite this weakness?

_____

_____

CHAPTER 14:
Investing in Your Energy

"It's not more hours you need; inject vitality into the hours you already have."
– Mofoluwaso Ilevbare.

There are majorly three primary sources of energy in the human body: thermal, chemical, and mechanical.[27] According to recent research, human energy is clean energy, and capable of powering portable devices and low-power electronic devices. What that tells me is there is so much potential and kinetic energy in your body. But it needs to be correctly understood. Consider these facts:

- We cannot generate more *time* but we can generate more energy.
- Time is finite; energy is infinite.
- Energy management is a science, but also an art.
- What gives you energy is different from what gives me energy.

---

[27] https://doi.org/10.1016/j.fmre.2021.05.002

- You are better at some things at some times of the day than at others.
- Every task takes a different amount of energy.
- You can reproduce energy and take charge of your well-being!

Learning to manage your energy holistically is key to vitality.

How to Harness Human Energy to Create Change in Yourself

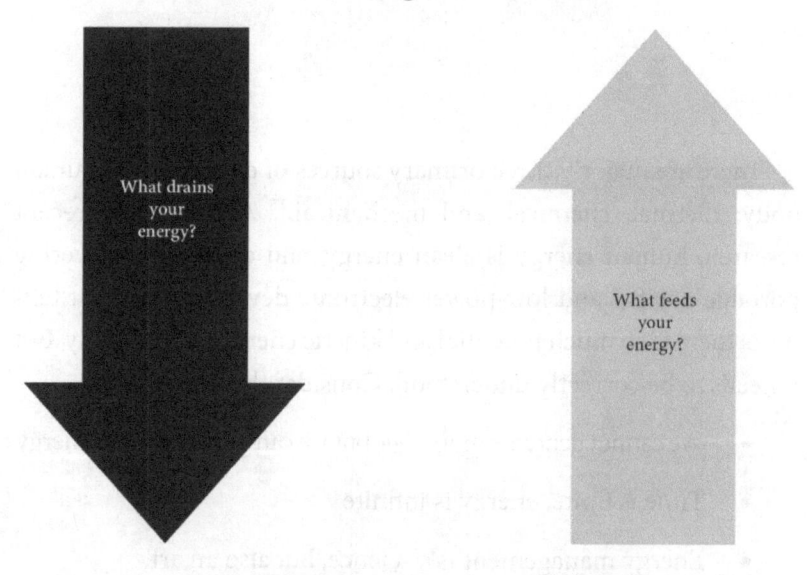

What drains your energy?

What feeds your energy?

You can't manage what you don't measure.
You can't change what you tolerate.

Consider the following table of scenarios and think about whether you find these to be energy giving or draining. Sometimes just thinking about these can cause stress; under other circumstances, the supposedly stressful scenarios can, in fact, be energising. The key is to understand yourself and identify what *you* find enhances or depletes your energy. Assess these scenarios and then give each a score of 1-5 on each side of the options, 1 being low and 5 being high. Caveat: you may feel like switching some items into a different column.

Scenario	Energy Draining	Energy Giving
Leadership	Dealing with high-pressure clients, decision-making, budgets, navigating organizational changes, team dynamics	Success and accomplishment, recognition, strategic planning, growth opportunities, new challenges, shaping company culture
Running a business	Managing day-to-day operations, handling challenges and teams	The satisfaction that comes from meeting consumer and customer needs, creating memorable experiences, improving health, happiness, and sustainability, creating wealth.

Family responsibilities	Balancing family needs, conflicts, and time management, schedules	Emotional support, bonding, fulfilment, sex, healthy food
Financial stability	Managing investments and financial decisions	Security, opportunities for personal and professional growth
Caring for aged parents	Emotional stress, bills, time constraints, sense of duty	Sense of duty, family connection, shared memories
Global challenges	Uncertainty, health concerns, adapting to remote work, travel	Resilience, adaptability, finding new opportunities
Health and wellness	Managing fitness routines, healthy eating, and mental well-being	Increased energy levels, improved focus, overall life satisfaction
Tech advancements and automation	Learning and adapting to new technologies, risk of becoming obsolete	Increased productivity, innovative opportunities, staying relevant
Pursuing further education	Balancing coursework, additional responsibilities	Intellectual growth, expanded skill set, future career prospects

Social media	Maintaining online business/personal brand, dealing with criticism	Money, connection with a wider audience, networking, recognition for expertise, partnerships and brand deals
Juggling multiple roles	Feeling overwhelmed, lack of work-life balance	Flexibility, personal growth, diverse experiences, bonding
Faith/church	Service and commitment bring fulfilment but can be time-consuming	Inner peace, purpose, joy, community support, hope
Community involvement	Commitment to social causes, time demands	Fulfilment, positive impact, networking opportunities

As much as we find fulfilment and joy in our energy givers, we all get tired from time to time. However, feeling constantly tired is not a normal feeling; if you do, you should get a medical checkup. Our bodies need energy to function. According to Morley Robbins[28], author of *Cure Your Fatigue: The Root Cause and How to Fix It On Your Own*, stress can deplete minerals in the body crucial for the

---

28 Morley Robbins, Cure Your Fatigue: The Root Cause and How to Fix It On Your Own

production of adenosine triphosphate (ATP), which pumps energy into the body cells so we can function well.

On a scale of 1–5, how energised do you feel in general and why?

Have you mastered habits that feed your energy?

The next phase of life will demand your energy, mostly in a good way. Your job, business, family, professional networks, social circles, pets, and even the traffic will demand energy from you. Without a routine for filling up your cup, there is a risk of fatigue and eventual burnout.

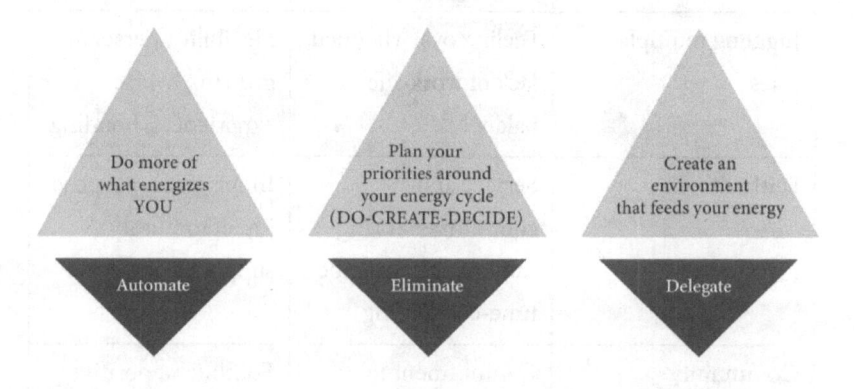

Do more of what energizes YOU	Plan your priorities around your energy cycle (DO-CREATE-DECIDE)	Create an environment that feeds your energy
Automate	Eliminate	Delegate

Just as you have to charge your phone or laptop after use, consider how you recharge yourself when your batteries are low. Where and what do you plug yourself into? The truth is that we cannot generate more than 24 hours in a day, but we can generate more energy and improve our productivity.

The problem is not *time* management, it is *energy* management. Time is finite, but energy is renewable. You don't necessarily need more time. You need more energy to maximise the time that you have and get the most important things done.

Feed Your Brain, Body and Mind

The brain controls our thinking, feeling, and decision making. That is not an organ you want to starve. Jim Kwik[29], a world-class brain coach and memory expert, talks about the importance of nutrition and certain foods to support cognitive health and brain performance. Examples of foods or fruits rich in antioxidants and that also have anti-inflammatory properties are avocado, blueberries, broccoli, eggs, turmeric, leafy green vegetables, beetroot, beets, coconut oil, nuts and seeds, salmon which is rich in Omega-3s fatty acids, and also dark chocolate in moderation, etc. What's your typical breakfast? How many times do you move your body per day? Build strength and stamina through walking, healthy exercise routines, nutrition, and other physical and mental well-being habits that suit your busy lifestyle.

Choose Your Battles

I try as much as possible to leave the house on a positive note. Sometimes when I'm at the airport or in a foreign country, I try to remember my last word or action before I left the house. As much as I trust God for safe travels, you never know if that moment could be your last. Give a hug, a kiss, a kind word to your loved ones before rushing off to the airport or dashing out for the day. Amy Clover reported in a HuffPost column[30] that researchers[31] have recognised that loving hugs have a positive influence on mental stability, self-esteem, anxiety, and blood pressure. Popularly known as the mother of family therapy, the late Virginia Satir[32] suggested:

---

29 https://www.jimkwik.com/
30 https://www.huffingtonpost.co.uk/entry/how-many-hugs-do-we-need-a-day_uk_64c8db6be4b021e2f2957950
31 https://www.happify.com/hd/8-reasons-why-you-need-at-least-8-hugs-a-day/
32 https://www.forbes.com/sites/christinecomaford/2020/08/22/are-you-getting-enough-hugs/?sh=7956ccd68dad

- four hugs a day = antidote for depression
- eight hugs a day = positive influence on mental health
- twelve hugs a day = positive psychological state

The reality is no one can adequately prescribe how many hugs you need or who exactly you should share that hug with. Hugs boost the release of the "happy hormone" oxytocin and can also give a feeling of safety. So, hug yourself, your pet, your kids, your spouse, friends, or that fluffy pillow. One unexpected incident can change your life forever, and the only thing you'd realize you really care about are the people in your life. When you're mad at your spouse but can't remember how the argument started in the first place, it's not worth brooding over. Make up quickly. Replace anger with love and bitterness with forgiveness. Cherish the moments, and choose peace and joy.

Spice up your Sex Life

My husband and I had a long-distance relationship for five years. This was because he was working as a seismic engineer mostly offshore in another country while I was still at the university. I'm talking about the era when a letter took 30 days to arrive and a response took about the same. When we finally got married, we opted to enjoy our first two years of marriage without having kids. That way we could catch up on enjoying each other's company and learn to live as a couple first. Sex was wild, warm, passionate, and as fun as it should be. After all, we were madly in love.

As time went by, we felt we were ready to welcome babies into our home, plus societal pressure started mounting. Alas, I couldn't get pregnant. Gradually, the spontaneous fun times spiralled into a sense of duty and anxiety, followed by a few years of emotional and psychological rollercoasters – monitoring ovulation cycles, scheduling sex dates, and dealing with devastating medical test results. My body suffered a lot.

After five years of waiting and another six years after that, we are blessed with two boys who are growing bigger by the day and who can clean out the food in the fridge in minutes. Fast forward to years after having kids, we've healed through the pain and grown in love. We had to be intentional and work our way back to a healthier, exciting level of intimacy. Healthy sex gives you energy – makes you feel alive – like it should. If you are in your happiest moments in your 40s, enjoy it. If you are newly married, nurture that relationship and shake things up every now and then. If you are single, consider what intimacy really means to you and how you want to have it work in future relationships.

Choose to be committed to your partner and keep the "fun dates" going. If you are feeling a little staleness in your marriage or experiencing hormonal changes, vaginal dryness, loss of libido, or chronic fatigue, communicate with your spouse and visit your GP. Help is available. Marriage should be enjoyed, not endured. If you are single and desire a loving partner, keep putting yourself out there, and I trust you will find a partner that complements you and helps you fulfil your purpose.

Live fully. Love Deeply. Care Wholly. Travel the world. Make the most of your strengths and aim for the best in your career. Appreciate the good things in your life. Expand your network and build legacies that will outlast you. We all deserve to enjoy the beauty that exists in the world around us.

EXAMPLES OF NATURAL ENERGY BOOSTERS

Sleep	Music	Hydration	Prayer
Balanced Meals	Acupressure	Breaks	Good posture
Breathwork	Less worrying	Tapping	Aromatherapy
Taking action	Feeling loved	Dancing	Family Get-Away
Journaling	Laughter	Herbal teas	Cold water
Money	Playing with Pets	Helping Others	A good book
Healthy gut	Optimism	Decluttering	Massage/spa
Mentors	Good hair	Smiling	Hugs

Form Strategic Alliances

During the COVID-19 pandemic, many businesses folded up, thousands of employees were laid off, and there was an unprecedented level of social isolation. Two years before that, my family and I relocated from Geneva back to Nigeria. Then, we relocated again from Nigeria to Australia for work reasons. About three months into our relocation, the COVID-19 pandemic erupted, disrupting the world as we knew it. With no close friends or family around us, and being a family of "huggers", it felt isolating. The neighbourhood was still strange, most of our personal belongings were still packed up in boxes in the garage, and I only had a few work colleagues I could call for support.

One of those days, over Zoom, while speaking with my long-time accountability partner who lived in the United States, we decided we would start an international virtual group for mid-senior professional women as a way of building strategic alliances and providing support for one another despite the geographical restrictions. We launched this platform we called Trailblazer Femme, and gave women on social media the opportunity to join us. Over a period of two and a half years, from 2021–2023, we supported 30+ paid members in junior and senior tiers, and about 1,000 women online with their personal and professional goals. Women joined us from across Africa, the United States, Canada, the United Kingdom, and Australia.

The premium members had monthly/quarterly accountability calls, set ambitious goals, and were mentored by guest speakers and coaches. Before that period was over, many of the women had concrete successes – promotions at work, dream jobs, speaking careers launched with booked speaking engagements, started non-profits, success in professional exams, became authors, embarked on international assignments – and found their true purpose (the real deal that makes them light up every day). We developed lifelong relationships and even wrote an anthropology together titled "Living Boldly – How to Transform From The Inside Out When Your Normal Shifts" where 10 co-authors shared strategies to live courageously through change. What are the odds that many of these successes could have happened in isolation from others? As life in the new normal began again, we officially dissolved the group yet, still today, these trailblazers continue to thrive in their goals and aspirations.

A strategic alliance is a deliberate partnership that leads to the co-development or exchange of capabilities and resources with mutual benefits. Continue to develop meaningful connections and expand your social and professional circles laterally, upwards, and downstream. For example, if you are a wealthy, successful business tycoon, look for other various business tycoons (aspiring, established, and benchmark), give back, and learn from them all. If you want to break into the world of AI and blockchain, seek out people with experiences to get on a faster learning track.

Do you have a networking schedule? Where could you go once a month to add value? In the next 90 days, whom do you need to know, and who needs to know you? Plan a 90-day visibility challenge (download the template in the Flourishing Forties Community vault). Find a few big Aunties and Uncles, too. Yes, you have become the big Auntie, but we all still need a Big Auntie too. Find your tribe and thrive together.

CHAPTER 15:
You're in the Driver's Seat Now

"Sometimes even the most exciting journey can be thwarted by a traffic jam, road accident, or unforeseen circumstances."
—*Mofoluwaso Ilevbare*

We were all excited when our older son celebrated his sixteenth birthday. His first wish was to sit for his learner's permit exam so he could get his freshly painted L plates and start driving lessons. He would finally enjoy the freedom that comes with being behind the wheel of a car. His younger brother was probably more excited for him – after all, having driven sports cars during gaming races, how difficult could it be to drive a physical car? The first time I got behind the wheel of a manual-drive car, I greatly anticipated the thrill of adventure. It took no time at all for me to realise it wasn't as easy as it looked.

Single tasking was not a framework built into those traditional cars. You had to be an expert at multitasking. With one foot on the accelerator, the other shuttling between the brakes and the clutch (if you learnt to drive with an automatic-drive, this would sound alien), both hands on the steering wheel, and occasionally one hand moving the gear shift... it felt like madness. *How come the rate of accidents was not rampant on the roads?*, I thought to myself. How could anyone learn to drive a car this way? I went home with mixed emotions that day.

The initial moments of learning how to drive any kind of vehicle can be challenging. I remember my elder sister driving our father's car into a ditch. For days, she wouldn't dare touch it. Her initial burst of energy was quickly replaced by frustration and disappointment.

The Rear-view Mirror

When I was learning to drive, I was taught how to reverse without turning my head but to use the rear-view mirror. This small part of the vehicle helps drivers monitor traffic and anticipate dangers, and gives visibility without the need to turn your head backwards. Drivers are advised to take a quick glance through the rear and side mirrors every 5–8 seconds to keep a mental map of the road and make better driving decisions. The rear-view mirror can be likened to a quick glance at your past/what's behind you. *A glance too long may prevent you from seeing what's ahead and cause an accident.* This is why many of us believe that learning from the past gives you a mental perspective of your mistakes and successes, but do not stay there! There are miles ahead to cover – keep your focus.

The Side Mirrors

"Objects in the mirror are closer than they appear" is commonly stickered on car mirrors. Frequent glances at the right and to the left mirrors give a driver a broader view of who's riding beside and behind you. The side and rear mirrors also help you sweep the area to assess any dangers and forecast who intends to overtake so you can give way. Picture a situation where there is a slow driver in front of you in the fast lane who won't bulge. It slows you down, doesn't it? Who are you taking on this journey with you, and how are you preparing for road blockers? Before you launch out on this journey, proactively check your "life side mirrors" and adjust the view for the best safety experience for you and other drivers on the roads of life.

The Steering Wheel

Recently, I watched a viral video where someone gave her grandfather a ride in a driverless car. The impulsive expressions and remarks exchanged between them during that short drive were hilarious. Who would have thought that such an experience would come so soon? Thanks to technology and genius creativity, autonomous cars, trains, and buses with partial-to-high automation capabilities are multiplying.[33] I must admit that I'm still resistant to trying out a self-driving car. Holding the stirring wheel and doing the simple jobs of braking and accelerating are tasks that give me a feeling of control. How easy is it to relinquish that? Imagine metaphorically driving through life in a driverless car – you would have to trust that the sensors are working perfectly, the path planning is in place, the global positioning system (GPS) tracking is

---

[33] https://www.thezebra.com/resources/driving/how-do-self-driving-cars-work/

mostly accurate, and the car knows how to avoid obstacles so it gets you safely to your destination.

The Control Pedals:

What a powerful force lies in the accelerator. As a car switches gears, the accelerator fires on, shortening the distance, speeding past slow runners, giving movement to your dreams. Think of the braking system. What would we do without brakes? Thank God, cars have brakes. No matter how fast and enjoyable life can be in the fast lane, there will come a time to apply the brakes. Red light. Green Light. Amber… all part of the process. Lastly, the transmission or gear box. Understanding the roles and limits of each pedal and how they communicate and are interconnected with the other parts of the vehicle ensures a functioning and safe vehicle.

Alignment and Balancing

Once you switch on the engine and get ready to drive, you find alignment in motion. A good driver knows how to steer the car safely, when to accelerate, when to make a U-turn, and when to bring the car to a halt, without causing a safety incident. As you drive, you keep a mental look out for distractions and other drivers on the road while obeying traffic regulations to get from one destination to another. When the wheels are out of balance or a car is overdue for maintenance, the driving experience can be unsafe and bumpy. Back in my high school days, I remember being in a taxi that seemed to constantly veer right even though I could see that the driver was steering straight.

Finding balance and enjoying life in your 40s can be likened to driving a car. You are in the driver's seat now. Not your parents, not your siblings, not your boss or customers, not even your past self. The present self, *you*! Have you ever driven absentmindedly to a different destination than intended only because your brain was on auto-pilot and used to that route? If yes, you may catch yourself saying "What was I thinking?"

Life as you know it is changing for the better. There are new bridges, shortcuts, and new roads that you will learn to drive on. The stronger your *why*, the more motivation and desire you will have to keep driving forward. The clearer your *destination*, the more laser-focused you are to get there. Road bumps on the way help us build resilience, while the rear mirror serves as a companion, not a constraint. How confident are you behind the wheel right now? Don't drive through your entire life in auto-pilot mode.

What If It Ain't Okay?

I'm a highly optimistic person who believes in being unstoppable. Sometimes, when people hear the word unstoppable, they assume it means everything always goes the way you want or you are always in motion, successful 24/7 all year round. But that would not be real life, would it? Life is a journey of twists and bends, bumps and smooth stretches.

How do you flourish when things are not okay? How do you take action and remain steady when you are going through change? Life will happen, and sometimes while you are in the driver's seat, the car may break down or require some maintenance to keep it healthy.

Breakdowns happen on the roads and in life generally, too. Cars break down unexpectedly on the road. Not necessarily only old cars; new ones with factory faults do, too. It can be stressful, especially if you have deadlines or find yourself in the middle of nowhere. What do you do when your car breaks down? A car website[34] suggested the following:

- Switch on your emergency lights (some call these hazard lights) for visibility and to alert other drivers around you that there is a problem. Learn to embrace vulnerability when you find yourself in an emergency situation, so it signals to others that you need help and can get the right support.

- If your car still works, steer it safely to the side of the road away from obstruction. In life, this can sometimes mean taking a break, getting out of the "doing" zone, or transitioning from headlines to sidelines, so you can assess the situation appropriately in a calmer state.

- Call the appropriate professionals for help. This is not the time to call your dentist or friend who cannot help. For times of crisis, have some emergency contacts stored on your mobile phone. Consider having a contingency contact list at home as well, which your kids may find handy.

- In a situation where your car is immobile, switch on the emergency lights, remain in your car, and call appropriate personnel for help – the police, tow truck, a reliable family member, or roadside assistance companies.

---

[34] https://www.dempstersqualitycarcare.com/blog/what-to-do-when-your-vehicle-breaks-down

Not Again!

With guns pointing to my face, the mad voice echoed down into the boson of my soul, "Come down from the car now!"

"*Not again!*" I muttered, my heartbeat racing.

I had recently been given a brand-new Honda Accord as part of my promotion package and was thrilled to drive the car around town. What a way to enjoy the fruits of years of hard work and dedication. On this fateful day, I was in our local church in Ibadan, Nigeria, for choir rehearsal. When we were done, feeling exhausted from the day's activities, a friend and neighbour of mine offered to drive since we were headed in the same direction.

A few minutes after we hit the road, it happened. We were trying to avoid a ditch when these strange-looking guys on motor bikes drove into our way. Unaware of who they were, we slowed down to avoid an accident, only for the driver and passenger to jump off the bike and point guns at us. Out of fear, my friend rationalised he could step on the accelerator and drive them off the road, but I said to him, "No, don't!"

He nodded repeatedly, already soppy with sweat.

"Remain still. Let's do as they say!" I said to him.

"*Oya, come down from the car!*" the robbers yelled.

We obeyed and came down from the car with our hands in the air: a sign of total surrender.

"*Who get this car?*" one of them asked.

"It belongs to me," I replied.

He took a few seconds to look at the car. It looked so posh and official.

"*Tracker dey this car?*" His voice sounded like it was forced from his throat — like someone who was drunk or high on drugs.

I replied, "No!"

"*What of security?*"

"No! It's a new car and we haven't installed anything yet."

At the signal of the gang leader, three of them went in and searched the car. Right there, they shoved us aside and drove off in my car while others followed. I was quite relieved that we weren't killed or kidnapped. Once again, God stepped in to deliver me from the hands of death. One of the lessons my father taught me when we were young was to memorize license plate numbers of our family cars. Coincidentally, earlier that fateful day, I had stared intensely at the license plate number of my new car and memorised it, not knowing that information was going to come in handy since our personal belongings, including wallets and laptops, were whisked off in the car. Passers-by and church members who came to our rescue were able to alert the police, who immediately sent an alert to neighbouring police stations and roadside checkpoints. Still shaken from the incident, we were driven home by someone else. I can't forget the look on my husband's face as I relayed what had happened.

Less than three hours after the incident, I received a call that the car had been recovered. From the story the police told me, the robbers had stripped my car of everything that was in it and handed it over to another man: an accomplice, of course, who had a police uniform and fake ID, a strategy that helped him to prevail at various checkpoints, except the last checkpoint at the border of the city.

Beyond that point, it would have been more difficult to trace. When the alleged driver got to this checkpoint, the police officers asked him for the car documents, which he failed to provide. Interrogation revealed something was amiss. Unknown to him was that a call had already been put through to all the police stations in the surrounding area, informing them of a stolen vehicle with the exact car's plate number he bore. He tried to bribe the police officers on duty, but they turned down his illicit offer and led him to the station. At the police station, it became clear that the car he was driving had been stolen and he wasn't who he said he was. He was arrested on the spot. We filled out the necessary papers, and after a few days, my car was released and handed back to me. What a day!

Who would have thought that such a beautiful gift from work could land me in another perilous situation? It made me wonder, "Why do bad things happen to good people?"

I used to think that the chances of evil happening to good people were very slim until I found myself in not one but three major crises in such a short life span. Having the consciousness that the issues of life are not peculiar to bad or good people enables you to position yourself with a positive outlook on life and expect the best of it. With the right attitude, you can handle whatever comes to you head-on. If you look back over the last four decades, have you lost something so dear to your heart that you ask the question, 'Why me?' It might be a loved one, a job, or a prized possession. Maybe you made bad decisions that caused your business to fold up. Or you've been treated unfairly which led to dire consequences.

I challenge you to start looking beyond 'Why me?'.

Let the pain of the past be a springboard to the possibility of a brighter future.

Lesson From the Ashes
What is one lesson from the ashes of your life that's built your resilience?

_____

_____

What's a silver lining you've anchored yourself on so far that will keep you going?

_____

_____

PART FOUR
Winter: Build for NEXT

The cycle of change

It is a fact
A deciduous tree will lose its leaves.
No matter how hard it tries to hold on
The cycle of life influences its form.

There is another fact
A deciduous tree can bloom again.
In sunlight's warmth, the roots take cue
The cycle of growth begins again.

Celebrate new life.
New fragrance in the air
Petals fluttering gently in the breeze
The cycle of change on branches once bare.

© Mofoluwaso Ilevbare

CHAPTER 16:
Laws of Nature

"We all go through rainy days. Whether you choose to dance in the rain or stay soaked is a mindset. It's not the presence of the rain that makes you dance. It's the hope that after the rain, comes a rainbow"
—Mofoluwaso Ilevbare

As each season turns, a deciduous tree goes through a transformation. For a season, the tree feels alive, blossoming with luscious leaves and a myriad of light – but hold on, autumn is lurking around the corner, forcing the tree to shed its leaves and make room for the new. Before it can stabilize, winter blows even harder, forcing its systems to retreat into a state of dormancy. Seemingly, on the outside, things seem to be dying. Still, on the inside, the tree is posturing, adjusting to the season's harshness on its naked body, building resilience, and consolidating nutrients because it knows there is another season to look forward to where new things will spring again.

Spring does return!

You may feel like it's nearly the end, but really our "third act" has a renewed season, and spring is once again simply another season for the older tree.

Have you ever felt so good in one season of life that you don't want it to pass? As that season rolls away, you may feel anxious, feel FOMO (fear of missing out), or feel you are being forced to retreat into a state of dormancy – a dormancy of ideas, hopes, and dreams. On the outside, others may critique or gossip in the corridors about your downward spiral. It is not for you to explain to everyone what you are going through.

During times of adversity, stress can be a catalyst for growth. Research tells us that the good kind of stress, called eustress, is good for us. You need a level of eustress or you lose the tension to expand and grow. No matter how juicy an orange looks, you cannot share in its goodness if you don't cut and squeeze it. The fruit comes from a flourishing tree, but it is useless to you without applying pressure. Whenever you are faced with harsh *winters* of life, ask for the capacity to grow through the tension.

In her article "The Secret Messages of Swaying Trees", British physicist Helen Czerski[35] describes with wonder the oscillating power of trees in the face of adverse winds. When strong winds blow in winter, the tree bends more easily due to its frailty. In the summer, the weight of the branches and leaves provides more stability. A deciduous tree needs a higher adversity quotient (the capacity to stay resilient in hardship situations)[36] during winter than in other seasons. What is your adversity quotient?

---

35 https://www.wsj.com/articles/the-secret-messages-of-swaying-trees-11574350152
36 https://saspublishers.com/media/articles/SJAHSS_1012_532-541.pdf

Trees adapt differently to seasonal changes. For example, the juniper tree produces antifreeze proteins, which help it withstand harsh weather conditions. The olive tree depends on its reserves, stored in the trunk, to keep metabolic activities going. The thornbush leverages its thorns to ward off herbivores, thus guarding its stored energy reserves. The oak tree sheds its leaves to reduce water loss. The beech tree undergoes winter embolism, preventing the water inside from freezing and destroying the tree. The bark of an aspen tree serves as an insulator during harsh temperatures. On the other hand, the Illawarra flame tree, native to Australia,[37] sheds its leaves in late spring or summer, which helps it conserve water during periods of reduced rainfall.

I've come to conclude that you get to choose whether this decade will be for you a *peak or a panic season*. After experiencing my share of winter seasons, I figured out the season would come around again at some point in life, so I took time to write down some lessons from my past experiences. I call them the S Laws.

The Law of Simplification

This law is rooted in the principle that *less is more*. We live in a world that screams "Buy me." You cannot watch a YouTube video for more than a few minutes without advertisements making you believe that your life is incomplete without that Rolex or AI-powered blender. It is why you rush to buy new clothes when seasons change, yet your wardrobe is already running over. The sales markups keep us hooked as if we need more stuff. You tell yourself, "I'll be happy when…", "I'll feel blessed when…".

---

[37] Care Tips For Illawarra Flame Tree (Brachychiton acerifolius) (thejunglecollective.com.au)

More is not always better. Less is. Less stuff, less worry, less baggage, less busyness. Travel light. Live light. Eat light. Like the deciduous tree, this season requires adversity tactics, and simplifying your life is smart. **Start with selective simplicity.** Choose three areas of your life to start with and gradually expand your focus to other areas once you've built the right habits. What can you simplify to set you up for your next season?

The Law of Silence

Researchers at John Hopkins University wrote that silence is not the absence of noise, meaning we can hear and perceive silence.[38] Other researchers have found that silence can raise your level of self-awareness, increase concentration, improve mood states, and promote well-being.[39] Building for the next one can be described as the silent season. In winter, deciduous trees go into dormancy as leaves fall off and internal energy is conserved. One of the skills you and I can develop as we mature is the ability to keep our mouths shut, even when we feel like blurting out everything. When my kids were little, they sometimes got me all worked up with their beautiful high-pitched tone, always asking questions or screaming around the house. We learned to play the "silence game". The goal was to see if we could all stay silent for ten or more minutes, and the first person to break the silence would lose the game. This was liberating – a simple way of finding some stillness in the chaos. Being highly competitive, my kids took the challenge seriously. I giggled quietly because it worked nine times out of ten. We probably kept this going for a few years before they outgrew it and didn't care as much about

---

38 (https://hub.jhu.edu/2023/07/11/can-we-hear-silence/).
39 (https://www.frontiersin.org/articles/10.3389/fpsyg.2020.00602/full)

winning. Researchers have pointed out that *"silence speaks though it says nothing, grows though it has no substance, hurts though it can touch nothing, and conceals though it cannot hide from perception"*.[40] Are you intentional about creating still moments in your day, week, or months?

The Law of Structure

The first time I watched a house being built from the ground up, I was astonished by the sheer volume of resources and work that went into laying the right foundations. Regarding foundations, there is one golden rule: *When you put something in the ground, it should not move.* [41]

In the previous chapters, I touched on the power of habits and how developing systems can enhance your productivity and provide structure for your life. In harsh economic situations, having a structure for managing your career, finances, relationships, priorities, and energy becomes very important. Conserving energy to cope with life and having a solid plan for your life can help you thrive through chaotic change.

When you sow a seed, you don't reap the seed. If that seed grows in good soil, you reap more than you sowed. In your moments of dormancy, multiply. Nurture the dreams you are about to birth, store up the nutrients you'll need for growth, rebuild, replenish, revitalize, and protect your future from external fires that could impact your naked, brittle branches in the winter season of life. Build resilience and strengthen your core in the quiet seasons so you are steady and balanced

---

40 (https://lmeinecke.com/downloads/pubs/OGrady-Meinecke-Silence-Too-Absent-to-Ignore.pdf).
41 https://practical.engineering/blog/2022/1/4/why-buildings-need-foundations

in the season of plenty. For a deciduous tree, the next spring's success could depend on how well it protects itself from dying by leaning into its less conspicuous parts.

Turning Full Circle

Drawing a circle requires downward, sideways, and upward movements. While spring and summer seem like "rising" seasons, autumn and winter seasons feel like "falling" seasons, but without them, there is no full circle. Every season serves a different purpose in the circle of life. Ready or not, change will happen. You can either let change happen *to you*, happen *for you*, or *in you*. Change can be subtle. When change happens quietly, it sometimes goes unnoticed. For change to last and be sustainable, it has to be powered by the level of courage and tenacity on your inside plus positive external reinforcements on the outside. In the downward moments of life, it may feel like while everyone else is climbing mountains and breaking boundaries, you are slipping and falling downwards, but for a tree to sustain itself, the roots must grow deep and find a steady stream of water and nutrients before the flourishing appears too.

> *"A deciduous tree cannot blossom in spring if, during winter, it hasn't gathered the resilience to thrive."* —Mofoluwaso Ilevbare

Make Room for the New

I went to a women's business retreat in Maui a few years ago. I met some amazing boss ladies, from army officers to beauty moguls. Over three full days, we delved into health, wealth, and influence strategies. The hunger for growth was tangible. We were all at different stages and different degrees of health, wealth, and influence. Whoever we felt we wanted to become or have at the next level, someone in the room had it.

There can be no manifestation of the new without some preparation. The new can create a disruption, and you must get ready to walk in it and embrace it. Anything that seems unfamiliar may be perceived as a threat. When we perceive a threat, our brain's natural reaction is a fright-or-flight response. This can create doubt and anxiety, shutting down your openness and flexibility to adapt.

One lesson I learned in that room was that as much as it is liberating to stand in confidence, own your power, and scream "I am good enough" affirmations every morning, it is also okay to recognize the moments you can confidently say "I am not good enough *yet!*" What a powerful rephrasing statement. It is not enough to say you are good enough and then settle for a life that feels safe and comfortable. When was the last time you did something for the first time? How often do you get the chills and thrills from being curious and adventurous?

Don't fall into the complacency trap! There is a demand on you to live your life to the fullest and change the world around you, no matter how small. Want to grow your business to a million dollars in revenue? Find someone who has done it and learn from them. Do you want to become the world's best podcaster or highest-paid speaker?

Find someone who's killing it on global stages and pay for mentoring. Do you want to pivot in your career and start from scratch? Find someone who has done it and humble yourself to begin again.

This decade is not the time to listen to one side of the story that says you are good enough. You are not done *yet!* There are still heights to reach, depths to dig into, rivers to cross, and horizons to build. The experiences and lessons I gathered in that room far away in "relaxing Hawaii" changed me, but it would never have happened if I didn't feel the need to grow.

You must prepare your *mind*.

You must prepare your *heart*.

You must prepare your *spirit*.

And you definitely must prepare your *body*.

The moment you accept there are some things you are not good at *yet,* you start to create room for growth. Yes, you'll suck at first. If you stop practising, you'll never get good at it. Your dreams will cost you something. But not dreaming costs you more. You cannot grow beyond the price tag you place on yourself. Your roots must go deeper and make room to increase your capacity for the new. Your branches must be ready for the sprouting of new leaves and make room for it. The environment into which the tree will expand has to make room for it.

Your dreams will cost you something. But not dreaming costs you more.

Fulfilling your purpose in life is tied to seasons. What you need to do in the blooming seasons may differ from who you need to become in the shedding seasons of your life. Understanding the present season you are in will help you prepare for the next, so that you are not caught unawares. Mind you, you can never be fully prepared, so why waste any more time? Sometimes, the season will require creating something new.

Coulda woulda shoulda…

Where there is alignment, change produces good growth.

- Who cares what you should have, could have, would have done by now?
- Who dictates where the sun should rise or set in your life?
- Who dictates which standards you measure yourself by?

Take chances. Look for opportunities. There will always be someone in a different season from yours, but many have gone through the season you are in. Recognize your season and be strategic about the systems and structures you implement. Do not keep patching the old with the new. There is growth in every season if you dig deep enough to look.

A Few Definitions to Remember

Regeneration: Change is inevitable. You can't stop the seasons changing but acknowledge and maximise them, as a gardener will nurture the trees through the seasons because they know each season benefits the overall growth. The more a tree bends in the wind, the more feminine it is, the more it bears fruit, it nourishes, and it protects.

Rebirth: The foundation for a tree is its roots. The roots are an anchor. If a tree suffers the loss of a branch or is cut down, the roots can continue to grow for a while, striving to find water and nutrients to stay alive so it can rebirth new branches and live.

***Resilience*:** Trees sway when pressured by wind or rain. Probably trees understand that standing still could cause breakage or damage to one of their parts and therefore reposition to weather the storm and still keep standing after the storm.

***Resolve*:** Healthy trees sway with beauty and grace in the wind. You can be that tree. Graceful in the storm. Bearing fruits to nourish others and being nourished itself. Your roots are deep and moist. As you nourish yourself, you nourish others and bring joy and shade with grace.

NOTE FROM THE AUTHOR

Hey Girlfriend,

As we conclude this transformative discussion, I want you to take a moment to reflect on the wisdom you've gained and the power you've reclaimed throughout these pages. The journey of womanhood through life is a remarkable one, full of twists and turns, changes and detours.

As I age, I am convinced that age is not a limitation; it is a testament to the richness of your experiences and the depth of your wisdom. The American entrepreneur and author Jim Rohn often said, "Don't wish it were easier; wish you were better."

As a woman in her 40s, I decided to write the kind of book I would want to read with some girlfriends at a book club – something another woman like me can relate to. Your 40s are not a time to shrink or hide; they're significant moments to rise, fly, and shine brighter than ever before. You've already overcome so much and emerged stronger than you thought possible. Now is your time to harness that strength and soar to new heights.

This decade is so significant because it gives you an opportunity to redefine, rediscover, and reimagine who you were called to be for the next two thirds of life (yes, you read me right – don't you dare call this midlife yet!). Stop hitting the snooze button on your life. No more waiting for the perfect moment or the right opportunity to live your best life. The time is now. Take that leap of faith, live purposefully, take care of your health, and embrace the fullness of who God created you to be. Regenerate something. Rebirth your dreams. Build resilience. Resolve to keep flourishing, no matter what!

As each year unfolds, as you work from a place of purpose, passion, and personal fulfilment, may you find the strength and grace to sway in the wind and finish strong.

You are standing on the edge of greatness, my friend.

- Acknowledge your worth.
- Recognise the strength that resides in you.
- Step into your power with confidence and conviction.
- Let go of societal expectations and age labels.
- Celebrate how far you've come.
- Radiate your light in a world full of darkness.
- Pursue your dreams with unbridled enthusiasm.
- Fearlessly embrace change.
- Be unapologetically and wholeheartedly a BETTER YOU!

Above all, remember to live with courage and compassion. For it is in these moments that we truly come alive and flourish. Poet and civil rights activist Maya Angelou once said, "Life is not measured by the number of breaths we take, but by the moments that take our breath away." Write to me and share your story at https://www.flourishingforties.com/stories

If there's one thing I encourage you to do, is to *take action*. I want you to take a moment right now – don't wait till tomorrow – and write down one action you will take in the next 30 days, and then for the next 3, 6, and 12 months. I hope that the thoughts in this book have given you wings to fly, strides to swim, and depths to explore. I raise my glass of lemon-infused water and celebrate you.

It's time to flourish and thrive!

Be unstoppable!

Dr Mofoluwaso Ilevbare

ONE LAST THING...

If you bought this book or were gifted it, take a selfie and tag @flourishingforties on social media. I would love to hear your feedback. Leave a comment on Amazon, Good Reads, or any online platform where this book is sold. It would mean a lot to me.

Would you like to be a podcast guest on our show and tell us how life is going in your 40s? I would love to hear about all the amazing strides and remarkable changes you experience in your business, career, and life.

It is a shame that not enough inspiring stories about women in their 40s are saturating the internet. No matter how big or how small, a win is always a win! I would love to collect authentic stories and share them on the Flourishing Forties blog to inspire and encourage more women like you.

You can join the movement. Your story fuels this movement and helps us spread the greatness and joy of flourishing in your 40s on your way to the golden 50s. Share your story today at https://www.flourishingforties.com/stories.

If you would also like to invite me to your virtual or in-person event, podcast guest interview, a conference keynote, or a media feature, reach out through my website. One of my team members will contact you promptly to coordinate the details.

Until I hear from you…Remember this

There is something extraordinary about you!

When the nights are cold, and you need some blanket

When the stakes are high, and you doubt your strength.

Remember this moment - the words on the pages of this book!

Choose to rise above the ashes - look ahead to new dreams

A whole new world awaits you – on the other side of 50.

Made in United States
Troutdale, OR
01/25/2025